Advance Praise
Shaping a

MW01094534

These conversations between two distinguished educators offer a host of interesting insights. Topics range widely, including prospects for Japan, China, and Hong Kong and reflections on the global economy and how it can more fully succeed for the world's populations. What shines through most vividly is a commitment to the value of humane education and an eagerness to explore what this entails amid the many challenges of the contemporary world.

—Peter Stearns, Provost Emeritus and University Professor, George Mason University

Shaping a New Society captures an insightful dialogue between two respected thought leaders, who interweave a cogent discussion of economics with a shared vision for a humanistic education. Organized around eight conversations, the discussion examines a wide range of issues that are at once historical and contemporary, backward and forward looking, and that tie together personal introspection with a far-reaching concern for society. Ikeda and Lau ground their exchange in wisdom that comes from scholarship, experience, and faith, to deliver with humility their hopes for a more prosperous, peaceful, and joyous world.

—Zeena Zakharia, Assistant Professor of International and Comparative Education, University of Massachusetts Boston

Shaping a New Society

Shaping a New Society

Conversations on Economics, Education, and Peace

LAWRENCE J. LAU
DAISAKU IKEDA

Dialogue Path Press
Cambridge, Massachusetts
2017

Published by Dialogue Path Press
Ikeda Center for Peace, Learning, and Dialogue
396 Harvard Street
Cambridge, Massachusetts 02138

© 2017 by Lawrence J. Lau, Soka Gakkai
All rights reserved
Printed in the United States of America

Cover design by Gopa & Ted2, Inc.
Interior design by Gopa & Ted2, Inc., and Eric Edstam

ISBN: 978-1-887917-18-6

Library of Congress Cataloging-in-Publication Data

Names: Lau, Lawrence J., 1944- author. | Ikeda, Daisaku, author.
Title: Shaping a new society : conversations on economics,
    education, and peace / Lawrence J. Lau, Daisaku Ikeda.
Description: Cambridge, Massachusetts : Dialogue Path Press, 2017. |
    Includes bibliographical references and index.
Identifiers: LCCN 2016059531 | ISBN 9781887917186 (pbk.)
Subjects: LCSH: Economic development—Social aspects. |
    Education—Social aspects. | Peace.
Classification: LCC HD82 .L289 2017 | DDC 306.3—dc23
LC record available at https://lccn.loc.gov/2016059531

10 9 8 7 6 5 4 3 2 1

About Dialogue Path Press

Dialogue Path Press is the publishing arm of the Ikeda Center for Peace, Learning, and Dialogue, and is dedicated to publishing titles that foster cross-cultural dialogue and greater human flourishing. Books published by the Center (including those produced in collaboration with other publishers before the establishment of Dialogue Path Press) have been used in more than 900 college and university courses. See back of book for details on Dialogue Path Press titles.

About the Ikeda Center

The Ikeda Center for Peace, Learning, and Dialogue is a nonprofit institution founded by Buddhist thinker and leader Daisaku Ikeda in 1993. Located in Cambridge, Massachusetts, the Center engages diverse scholars, activists, and social innovators in the search for the ideas and solutions that will assist in the peaceful evolution of humanity. Ikeda Center programs include public forums and scholarly seminars that are organized collaboratively and offer a range of perspectives on key issues in global ethics. The Center was initially called the Boston Research Center for the 21st Century and became the Ikeda Center in 2009.

For more information, visit the Ikeda Center website: www.ikedacenter.org

Table of Contents

Lawrence J. Lau (left) and Daisaku Ikeda, Tokyo, 2007

CONVERSATION ONE

Economics for the People

IKEDA: I am delighted to have this opportunity to engage in dialogue with you, Professor Lau. You have been a source of sound policy advice on major trends in the world economy as a distinguished economist in key posts in numerous academic institutions, including as the sixth vice chancellor (and president) of the prestigious Chinese University of Hong Kong. I wholeheartedly welcome our exchange of ideas focused on such topics as economics, education, and issues specific to Asia.

My first meeting with you made a profound impression on me. You and I had the opportunity to share our thoughts when you visited the Seikyo Shimbun Building in Tokyo on the evening of January 16, 2007, an occasion that deepened our friendship, which I have cherished ever since.

In October 2007, you further honored us with your visit to Soka University in the suburbs of Tokyo, where you delivered a masterful lecture titled "The Chinese Economy: Opportunities and Challenges." The lecture greatly stimulated the intellectual curiosity of the Soka University students and stirred their desire to learn more.

LAU: Thank you very much, President Ikeda. It is my great honor and privilege to engage in dialogue with you and to learn from your great wisdom and vast experience. I have of course known of your distinguished name and that of your organization, the Soka Gakkai, as well as your many varied accomplishments in different fields for a long time, even while I was still teaching at Stanford University, long before I returned to Hong Kong to assume the presidency of CUHK and long before I had the honor of meeting you.

To me, you were best known for your steadfast and tireless advocacy of disarmament, especially nuclear disarmament, and peace around the world, and for your pioneering and unwavering efforts in promoting friendship and understanding between the peoples of China and Japan, indeed, even between the governments of the two nations.

I also learned of the long-standing close and cordial relations between you and CUHK, dating back to the time of our founding vice chancellor, Professor Li Choh-ming, and between Soka University, which you founded, and our university. CUHK is very proud indeed to count you as one of our most distinguished honorary alumni.[1]

As you know, Soka University is one of the first universities around the world with which CUHK established a regular, ongoing, academic exchange program, beginning in 1975. Now, after almost forty years, the exchange program between the two universities is still going strong.

IKEDA: CUHK was the first university with which Soka University reached an exchange agreement. In 1975, four years after the founding of our university, CUHK opened its doors to exchange with us, and for this we shall be eternally grateful. Today, Soka University has entered into exchange agreements with more than 140 universities throughout the world, and we are honored by the recognition CUHK extended us at the start of our journey. In addition to faculty and student exchanges, we have established a strong record of exchange between our two institutions in the areas of scholarship, culture, and other fields.

I have visited CUHK on four occasions—in 1974, 1983, 1992, and 2000—and have fond memories of engaging in dialogue not only with your faculty and staff but with your students. In 2006, we were fortunate to have CUHK cosponsor the well-attended Hong Kong stop of the touring exhibition *The Lotus Sutra—A Message of Peace and Harmonious Coexistence* with the Institute of Oriental Philosophy, which I founded, and the St. Petersburg branch of the Institute of Oriental Studies of the Russian Academy of Sciences.[2]

I understand that you took time from your busy schedule to come and view the exhibition, which was held at the Soka Gakkai International of Hong Kong Culture Centre. On that occasion, you brought a gift for me—a work of your maternal grand-uncle, whom you affectionately refer to as "grandfather," titled *Master of Cursive Calligraphy: Yu Youren 1879–1964*. I prize it to this day as a great cultural treasure.

In addition to being an eminent calligrapher, Yu Youren was a well-known revolutionary leader and close friend of Sun Yat-sen. He was also an outstanding educator, poet, and politician, and traveled to Japan, where, I have heard, he first met Sun Yat-sen.

When did you first visit Japan, Professor Lau?

LASTING PEACE IN ASIA

LAU: I still remember vividly my very first visit to Japan. It was in the summer of 1961. I was on my way to the United States to begin my studies at Stanford University. I had just spent a couple months in Taipei, visiting with my family (my mother, unfortunately, had passed away the year before). Both my paternal grandfather, Liu Hou-wu, and my maternal grandfather, Yu Youren, had come to the Taipei airport to see me off, and that was the last time I saw my grandfather Yu.

Later, I was invited by some close family friends of my father's who lived in Tokyo to spend a couple weeks with them in Japan on my way to the United States. Their home was in Shinjuku Ward. At the time, as far as I can remember, Shinjuku was completely flat—there were no tall buildings there at all. My father's friends took me around Japan, and I visited many places—Hakone, Kamakura, Nikko, and of course Mount Fuji.

The Japanese people left deep impressions on me. They are unfailingly courteous, absolutely law-abiding (or rather, rule-abiding), and extremely professional, in the sense that they try to do perfectly whatever they are responsible to do, no matter how trivial the tasks may appear to others. They specialize in what they do and are totally dedicated to their specialties and never, ever, take shortcuts. (Those who have attended Japanese tea ceremonies will understand perfectly what I mean.) They also possess a degree of civic consciousness and national solidarity that are rarely found elsewhere. Each subsequent visit I made to Japan just reinforced my initial impressions.

I am not alone in being most impressed with the degree of social order and cohesion displayed by the Japanese people after a major disaster such as the devastating 2011 Tohoku earthquake and tsunami.[3]

IKEDA: We in Japan are profoundly grateful for the messages of encouragement and the assistance sent from China and many other countries around the world, including from individual donors, at the time of the earthquake and tsunami. They provided us with immeasurable encouragement, for which I once again offer my appreciation. In the years since the calamity, we have reaffirmed our vow to forge on in the recovery and reconstruction process as we cherish the human bonds that bring us together in the spirit of mutual support.

I am surprised to learn that your first trip to Japan was in 1961, the same year as my first visit to Hong Kong. That was the year after I was inaugurated as third Soka Gakkai president at the age of thirty-two, a time when I was extremely busy with my new duties. I traveled to six countries and territories in Asia from January 28 to February 14, 1961. Hong Kong was the first stop on my itinerary.

Ever-present in my mind was the wish of Josei Toda, my mentor and the second president of the Soka Gakkai, to open a way to the happiness and lasting peace of all the people of Asia. During World War II, Mr. Toda was incarcerated for two years at the same time as his mentor, Tsunesaburo Makiguchi, the founding Soka Gakkai president, because of their opposition to the policies of Japan's militarist government. Makiguchi, who was quite advanced in age, died in prison. When Toda was eventually released, he carried on his mentor's spirit, striving to impart hope and courage to people through Nichiren Buddhism while broadening the reach of our grassroots movement to advance peace and humanitarian service. He often shared his belief that Japan would only be seen as a peaceful nation when she won the trust of her fellow Asian countries.

When I arrived at Kai Tak Airport on my visit to Hong Kong, about ten local Soka Gakkai members were awaiting me. That evening, I attended a discussion meeting, which marked the first modest step taken by the HKSGI, as it is known today, to promote peace, culture, and education based on Buddhism.

After Hong Kong, I traveled to Ceylon (present-day Sri Lanka), India, Burma (Myanmar), Thailand, and Cambodia, before returning to Hong Kong, from which I flew back to Japan. The numerous trips for peace in Asia I have made since that time always began and concluded with stops in Hong Kong. It is a special city for me.

I am interested to learn that your father's friends lived in Shinjuku, and that you visited them there. Shinjuku was the first place you stayed in Japan, and, as you know, the Soka Gakkai headquarters is in Shinjuku, and I am a local resident. I cannot help but feel a mystic bond in this.

Be that as it may, the Japan you experienced on your first visit to the country had at last recovered from the war and was entering a period of rapid economic growth.

Lau: I believe it is a sign of the success of the Japanese social and educational system that Japan has been able to modernize itself and yet still preserve most of its cherished cultural and social values. Indeed, Japan is the only country that has managed to do so. The Chinese have tried maintaining Chinese values at the core and adopting Western science for applications since the late-nineteenth century, but they have not really been successful thus far.

I also remember vividly my first meeting with you in Tokyo in January 2007. I was most impressed then with your masterful grasp of the affairs of the world and your deep knowledge of history, art, economics, literature, poetry, science and technology, and other social sciences, in addition to religion. You are an intellectual giant of the world.

I was also greatly honored to receive an honorary doctorate from Soka University of Japan that year. I enjoyed very much my visit to Soka University and meeting the faculty and students there. I was given such a warm welcome that it was almost like coming home. I am very proud indeed to have become an honorary member of the worldwide Soka community.

The Asian Financial Crisis

Ikeda: You are too kind. We were absolutely thrilled to welcome such a globally renowned economist to Soka University.

Economics is not my specialty, but its importance was deeply impressed upon me when I was young. In the summer of 1947, two years after the war ended, I was nineteen when I first encountered Mr. Toda. From that time until his death, over the course of ten years, he not only taught me the faith upon which I would base my life but mentored me in the skills needed to successfully overcome the tribulations of our world and tutored me in a wide range of subjects. One of the first subjects he prioritized was economics. We began in the early 1950s, and the textbook we used was *Keizaigaku nyumon* (Introduction to Economics) by Kanae Hatano, published in 1950 by Nihon Hyoron Sha, a widely recognized work. Being a businessman, Mr. Toda placed great importance on studying economics, insisting that a person who lacks a firm grasp of the subject could neither accomplish great things nor become a first-rate leader.

There are numerous theories concerning the etymology of the Japanese word for economics, *keizai*, but it seems to have derived from a classical Chinese phrase, "manage society for the welfare of the people." The English word *economy* derives from the Greek *oikonomia*, meaning "household management." Economics can thus be said to have originated from the question of how to most wisely manage our affairs—precisely the question that our society seeks to answer today.

Given this, I hope that our dialogue can serve as a class in economics for me, so that you can teach me how it will enable ordinary people to fulfill their aspiration to lead better, happier lives. In addition to your specialization in economics, I look forward to discussing with you humanistic education; issues relating to Hong Kong, China, and Asia; and our visions of a brighter future for the entire human race. You possess the expansive acuity to address such issues. I believe that engaging in dialogue with individuals of exceptional insight and achievement, and leaving a record of their thoughts, is an invaluable, fruitful endeavor in life.

LAU: In this, you should be my teacher, and it is I who should be asking you questions.

IKEDA: Not at all. Let me start by asking you several questions about economics. The period from the end of the twentieth into the beginning of the twenty-first century was one of dizzying change for the global economy. Starting in Thailand in September 1997, a currency crisis arose—often referred to as the Asian financial crisis or the East Asian currency crisis.[4] The sudden, rapid devaluation of many currencies in the region was a seriously debilitating influence on the economies of Asian nations. Major financial institutions in Japan at the time fell under extreme duress as well, and the International Monetary Fund had to intervene in Thailand, Indonesia, and South Korea in order to rebuild their economies.

Professor Lau, you predicted the 1997 Asian financial crisis and raised the alarm two years prior to its occurrence—a feat that garnered widespread acclaim.

LAU: Yes, I did predict the 1997 East Asian currency crisis back in 1995, at a World Meeting of the Project LINK, which was led by Professor Lawrence R. Klein, Nobel laureate in economic sciences, in Pretoria, South Africa. I repeated my prediction in 1996 at a conference in Beijing, in the presence of the governor of the People's Bank of China, the central bank of China. I did not predict the actual time of the crisis but simply identified it as something waiting to happen for such economies as South Korea and Thailand. Unfortunately, my prediction did come true, and the people of many East Asian countries and regions suffered great hardships.

IKEDA: It was an important historical lesson. The truth hurts, as they say. All too often, even when a crisis is looming, people find it difficult to accept the truth, or they refuse to give a fair, honest hearing to ideas that go against the tide of the times. This is one of the chronic failings of human society, unchanging throughout history. Such failings remain with us to this day, as evidenced by the emergence of negative aspects to global capitalism and the escalation in the "money games" of speculative investment.

In 2008, the US investment bank Lehman Brothers Holdings, Inc., collapsed, and the resulting shock quickly spread to financial markets throughout the world, bringing to mind for many the Great Depression, which started in 1929, when I was an infant. The world economy was gripped by a crisis described as occurring once in a century.

As I understand it, while the crisis was ostensibly triggered by the failure of Lehman Brothers, its roots go much deeper to the overheating of the US housing market that began around 2000 along with its associated subprime loans.[5] Subprime loans targeted lower-income borrowers; these mortgage loans were initially offered at low interest, but the rates would rise after a certain time. Many borrowers used subprime loans in the hope that their homes would increase in value in what appeared to be a bull market.

Unfortunately, the housing bubble burst, and the collateral value of homes imploded as real estate values collapsed, causing thousands upon thousands of homeowners to default on their loans. Lenders could not recover the money they loaned because the foreclosed homes they repossessed were worth much less than the original loans—and, once loans were foreclosed, lenders no longer received income (including interest on the loans) from the borrowers, rendering the loans nonperforming.

The situation was exacerbated by investment banks and other financial institutions that packaged subprime loans with other financial instruments (securitization) and sold them in world markets as new financial products. As the US housing market crumbled, so did the ratings of the mortgage-backed products, and their value consequently plummeted.

Saddled by the enormous holdings of such financial products,

Lehman Brothers and other institutions were hit by huge losses and eventually forced into insolvency. A chain reaction of mistrust and anxiety spread rapidly, and financial institutions stopped investing and lending, severely crimping the flow of money around the world and bringing on the global financial crisis.

Did you see this crisis coming?

The Global Financial Crisis

LAU: I cannot say that I foresaw the severity of the global financial crisis of 2007–09 in the same way that I predicted the 1997 East Asian currency crisis. But back in early 2007, before the failure of the subprime mortgage loans and the bonds backed by them in the United States, I noticed that the spread between the yields on junk bonds and US Treasury bonds of the same maturity had narrowed considerably, to less than 100 basis points. I thought that was impossible and unsustainable, and that the market must have misjudged the risks of the junk bonds. No matter how clever one is in financial engineering, risks can only be diversified, spread around, and shared—they could not have disappeared altogether.

The fact that they seemed to have disappeared altogether indicated that something was very wrong with the bond market, that there was serious underpricing of the junk bonds relative to the Treasury bonds, and that the rating agencies must have been mistaken. And if junk bonds were underpriced, because of the compression of the interest rate spreads, other bonds, including mortgage-backed bonds, must also have been underpriced.

Unfortunately, my premonition turned out to be correct. But I did not foresee the magnitude of the global financial crisis.

IKEDA: That which entails high risk customarily necessitates high interest. Yet, when the spread between yields on high-risk junk bonds and low-risk country bonds grew narrower, you realized that there was something wrong with the market.

When Lehman Brothers collapsed, there were some in Japan who took the optimistic view that the problem would be confined to the US economy, but they were wrong, and Japan was also pitched into an economic crisis. In today's globalized market economy, the financial threat caused by the bursting of the US housing bubble did not remain restricted to a single nation but had a dire influence on people all around the world. This, I take it, is the lesson of the collapse of Lehman Brothers.

Some say the new possibility that a worldwide depression, previously regarded as a once-in-a-century event, can occur at any time is a salient feature of the modern age. That humanity must constantly live in the shadow of another economic disaster of similar magnitude—this is the stark, unadulterated truth as long as we live in such a global economy. The economic crises in Greece[6] and other nations reported in the news recently can no longer be regarded as some distant events unrelated to our own lives.

We have witnessed the bursting of bubble economies in the past and the grievous harm they have wrought. Is there any way to prevent the destructive effects of such speculative economic phenomena and the collapses they cause?

LAU: What caused the global financial crisis of 2007–09? The principal causes were: (1) easy money in the United States; (2) failures of regulation and supervision; and (3) defects in the institutional design of the financial sector.

Why were these serious regulatory failures possible?

Regulatory failures have manifested in many areas since 2007, principally: (1) unwillingness and inability to restrain irrational exuberance; (2) excessive leverage of financial institutions (as well as some nonfinancial firms) and of the financial sector as a whole; (3) failure to ensure competitive markets; and (4) failure to control moral hazard.

Irrational exuberance is not uncommon—economic bubbles have occurred from time to time all over the world for centuries, driven by (initially) self-fulfilling asset price expectations and abetted by the heavy use of leverage. However, bubbles can and should be contained and restrained by suitable and timely restrictions on the use of leverage.

I believe that the global financial crisis of 2007–09 was exacerbated by serious mismanagement on the part of US policymakers, especially after the first half of 2008, including the handling of the Lehman Brothers case. The damage resulting from the global financial crisis could certainly have been better contained if the right actions had been taken.

THE MONEY GAME

IKEDA: The relationship between nations and markets is an important point of discussion in modern economics, isn't it? What you're saying is that, had the US government taken the appropriate measures to effectively curtail the impact of the Lehman collapse, the outcome could have been far different.

LAU: Yes. If bubbles are left entirely to the market, they will certainly eventually burst, but then they will have become much bigger and will therefore do much greater damage to the economy. Pricking a bubble early actually protects the investors who are the least knowledgeable and are often the last to enter the market and hence are "left holding the bag."

Recovery of an economy from a burst asset price bubble can take years or even decades. The collapse of the Japanese real estate market in the early 1990s is an example. The real estate price bubble in Hong Kong is another example. Prices of Hong

Kong real estate reached a peak in late 1997, after, not before, the handover of sovereignty from the United Kingdom to China; but then, prices fell by almost 60 percent and did not recover to the 1997 levels until 2009–10.

IKEDA: Even though the financial instruments related to subprime loans were clearly high-risk products, the risks were drastically underestimated when they went on the market, creating an untenable situation. In the process, certain individuals reaped enormous profits, while other investors, who lacked access to accurate information, suffered horrific losses.

It was certainly a time when the speculative "money game," nothing short of deviant, was allowed to run rampant. And its egregious effects were felt even by those in no way involved in the "game." Despite the fact that no discipline is more critical to our collective lives today than economics, many feel that the occasions when it actually proves useful are increasingly rare.

The economist John Kenneth Galbraith once shared with me his view that economics has drifted from reality probably because many economists cling to outdated theories. And it is precisely because the world is fraught with uncertainty that we should search for trustworthy guides and protocols to inspire us with the hope and confidence needed to advance into the future. This is another reason I feel this opportunity to learn from an insightful, well-grounded economist like you is so meaningful.

LAU: I have already identified the major mistakes of both the financial institutions and the regulatory and supervisory agencies. But I believe the problem, at its most fundamental level, is the deeply and strongly held belief that the freer the economy, the fewer restrictions, the better, and that not only can the free market do no wrong, it will also lead to the best social outcome.

I believe in the market mechanism, but I do recognize that in

order for it to lead to the best outcome, it must meet certain conditions, and these conditions cannot and will not be automatically fulfilled without appropriate regulation and supervision. The
market can often fail, for various well-known reasons. When it
fails, it is most often the common people who bear the heaviest
burden of that failure, and the government (taxpayers) that winds
up stepping in to pick up the pieces.

To overcome the current crisis, the developed economies must
focus on restarting the real economy[7] on a path of sustainable
growth and not on inventing additional financial wizardry. One
must not lose sight of the fact that the role of the financial sector is
to support the other sectors of the economy, and that, ultimately,
the financial sector must be based squarely on the performance of
the real economy itself.

There are limits to financial engineering—a bad risk remains
ultimately a bad risk no matter what one does. A financial sector
that is based on the performance of the financial sector alone is a
mirage, a bubble, and cannot sustain itself.

Unfortunately, Wall Street does not seem to have learned the
lesson. However, the strength of the US economy lies in its capacity to innovate. I believe innovation will resume, investment will
increase, unemployment will decline, albeit gradually, and pro-
ductivity will rise. The United States will, in time, start growing
normally again and hopefully will not repeat its financial excesses.

CONVERSATION TWO

Hong Kong's Potential

IKEDA: Let us now turn to Hong Kong, which continues to serve as an important global economic and financial center for Asia and the world. It is also a city of enormous appeal and dynamism.

Whenever I visit Hong Kong and come into contact with the enthusiasm of its people, their lack of pretense, and the tremendous energy engendered by their openness and vitality, I feel invigorated. In this, I believe the people there are similar to the people of the Kansai region of Japan, with whom I shared many joys and sorrows in my youth. This one reason I find Hong Kong so endearing.

You were born in Zunyi in Guizhou Province, China. How did you become connected with Hong Kong?

LAU: As you note, Hong Kong is not my birthplace, but I lived there from 1947 to 1961, from age two until I left Hong Kong to pursue university studies in the United States at age sixteen. I attended two years of kindergarten, six years of primary school, and five years of secondary school in Hong Kong (all at St. Paul's

Co-educational College). In other words, I spent all my formative years in Hong Kong. So even though Hong Kong is not my
birthplace, I have strong emotional attachments to it and consider
myself to be from Hong Kong.

IKEDA: How would you sum up Hong Kong's appeal?

LAU: What gives Hong Kong its special charm and appealing
character is its openness. It is readily accepting of success, especially monetary success, and pedigrees do not count much. Hong
Kong people have shown themselves to be highly adaptable, flex-
ible, and pragmatic. Hong Kong people are first and foremost
survivors.

IKEDA: Yes, I see what you mean. It has already been seven-
teen years since Hong Kong reverted to China in 1997.[1] Before
the reversion, the prevailing predictions regarding Hong Kong's
future were dire. Many were worried that once it came under
Chinese rule, all of its government policies would be changed, its
freedoms would be significantly restricted, and it would lose its
appeal and strength as a free port open to all.

   I had always felt that the reason for Hong Kong's dramatic
growth and development was the hope that surges through its
people—a belief that was confirmed after I spoke with a large
number of leading figures who live there, as well as the HKSGI
members.[2] As long as that spirit remained alive, I was certain, a
positive way forward would be found. As a result, I saw a bright
future for Hong Kong and maintained that Hong Kong's continued growth and development were unshakeable.

   In meetings with the successive governors of Hong Kong while
it was still under UK administration, as well as with prominent
members of the Chinese government, I communicated my beliefs

with utter candor. Senior leaders in China consistently assured me that they intended to preserve Hong Kong's prosperity.

The "one country, two systems" approach currently being followed, in which Hong Kong is a Special Administrative Region[3] with a prospering capitalist economy within the larger Chinese socialist system, is a unique experiment in human history. Looking back over the years since Hong Kong's reversion to China, a large number of Hong Kong residents who had once emigrated to Canada and other countries before the reversion have returned to Hong Kong. I believe this shows that Chinese efforts regarding Hong Kong have met with success.

LAU: I also view very positively the return of Hong Kong to Chinese sovereignty. I believe it is actually supported not only by the Chinese people on the mainland but by Chinese people everywhere, including even those who are anti-communists. Even Taiwan sent a delegation to witness the handover ceremony on June 30, 1997.

Almost all Chinese people, regardless of political persuasion, regard the Opium War treaties of 1842, which ceded Hong Kong to the United Kingdom, and 1860, which ceded a portion of the Kowloon Peninsula to the United Kingdom, as unequal treaties entered into under duress and hence not legally binding. In a sense, the return of Hong Kong to Chinese sovereignty in 1997 was overdue, considering that almost all of the other former British colonies in Asia, Africa, and elsewhere were granted independence in the 1960s.

IKEDA: Historically speaking, the return of Hong Kong to Chinese sovereignty can be seen as an inevitability.

I have visited China numerous times and have many dear friends both there and in Hong Kong. The HKSGI members are striving to contribute to the prosperity of Hong Kong as model citizens. It is my hope that events will continue to move in the most beneficial direction for the prosperity of both Hong Kong and mainland China.

RETURN TO CHINA

LAU: However, there were all sorts of doomsayers predicting that Hong Kong would be finished after its return to Chinese sovereignty. One only has to read magazines such as *The Economist* and *Fortune* that were published at the time.

I was one of the few economists who predicted a smooth transition in 1997. Today, one would have to agree that the reversion to Chinese sovereignty was successfully implemented. Life in Hong Kong has basically continued as before. The people of Hong Kong have continued to enjoy the same civil liberties. And, if anything, the voices of the people are now heard more loudly and more often than before 1997.

IKEDA: According to the Index of Economic Freedom announced in January 2014, Hong Kong topped the world for twenty consecutive years, including the years since its reversion to China in 1997. Hong Kong also managed to overcome the arduous challenges created by the East Asian currency crisis, which occurred at roughly the same time as its reversion, while keeping the impact of the severe acute respiratory syndrome (SARS) epidemic in 2003 to a minimum.

These were followed by the global crisis of 2007–09 that was brought on by the US financial crisis, and more recently, international uncertainty in the face of the lingering debt crisis in Europe. Yet even in these circumstances, Hong Kong has continued to achieve steady growth. As China assumes greater importance in the global economy, Hong Kong's role as an international financial center is certain to grow more important.

LAU: Hong Kong has much greater opportunities as a part of China than it did as a British colony. It can play a much greater role in the development and modernization of China and benefit accordingly. Hong Kong, if it had remained a British colony, would have fared much worse in the crises that affected it since July 1, 1997. During the East Asian currency crisis, the SARS crisis, and the more recent global financial crisis, Hong Kong could emerge relatively unscathed principally because of the support provided by the Chinese government in various ways.

The rapid growth of the mainland Chinese economy and its international trade, together with the resulting demands for financial, logistical, transportation, and other professional services that it is able to generate for Hong Kong, has become a mainstay of its economy. Had Hong Kong remained a British colony, the United Kingdom would have been both unwilling and unable to support the economy of Hong Kong to anywhere near the same extent.

Looking ahead, the real GDP of the mainland Chinese economy is likely to equal that of the United States in real terms before 2030. Hong Kong should try to take full advantage of China's economic growth by integrating its economy more closely with Shenzhen in Guangdong Province and southern China. Given the complementary economies of these regions, there are plenty of opportunities for win-win economic collaboration and cooperation.

IKEDA: I believe the changes brought on after Hong Kong's reversion extend beyond its economic ties with the mainland—it has affected not only people's daily lives in Hong Kong, China, and other places, but also their perceptions. For example, according to one study, a growing number of students from China studying abroad seek to establish residence in Hong Kong upon completion of their overseas study. It appears that they are drawn to Hong Kong because of its continued identification with China's cultural norms and its sense of openness as a gateway city to the world, as well as its economic freedoms.

In another survey, some 40 percent of Hong Kong respondents, when asked what their nationality was, said they were Chinese—the most people who have felt this way since Hong Kong was returned. Such shifts in public attitudes, I feel, deserve closer attention when examining Hong Kong's future prospects. In particular, I believe that any examination of Hong Kong's development in the years to come should fundamentally address not only the economic challenges but educational issues as well. After all, education is what shapes people's minds and anchors their identities, and it is people who play a decisive role in shaping the future.

Drawing on your rich experience as an educator, what is the present state of higher education in Hong Kong, and what are the challenges it faces?

OVERCOMING SELF-CENTEREDNESS

LAU: In Hong Kong, there is complete and total academic freedom in all of the tertiary educational institutions—including the nine publicly supported and two private universities. There is also complete and total freedom of speech on the university campuses. Opinions of all persuasions, political and otherwise, are freely expressed. And no one is spared from criticism, including even the chief executives of the Hong Kong Special Administrative Region.

When I served as the president of CUHK, I was routinely criticized by some student groups and even some alumni groups through large posters or demonstrations on campus. In my view, the university administration's proper role is, first and foremost, to maintain complete political neutrality, so as not to discourage the free expression of any opinion by anyone on campus. And second, to make sure that all voices, whether "politically correct" or not, can be heard, and that no one group, no matter how large or loud it may be, is allowed to prevent others from expressing opinions different from its own.

IKEDA: I have often heard of the remarkable growth and advancement that have been achieved by CUHK through the efforts of its administration, faculty, and students. As an honorary member of your university, nothing could make me happier.

The passion for education displayed by Hong Kong people and indeed the Chinese in general is well known. In Japan, an attempt was made in 2002 to revise educational policy and thus ameliorate the deleterious effects of the fiercely competitive examination system to enroll in the best schools. The new, less-intensive approach became the object of criticism, as academic aptitude levels of Japanese students declined in comparison to other countries, and was discontinued after some ten years. The direction now has shifted once again toward long hours of instruction. The goal is to place as much emphasis on the purpose of learning as raising scholastic aptitude.

According to the Programme for International Student Assessment conducted by the Organisation for Economic Cooperation and Development, Hong Kong students consistently rank among the top performers. In 2012, for example, Hong Kong was second in reading, third in math, and second in science.[4]

LAU: Chinese parents still value education as much as their ancestors did, and Chinese families in Hong Kong are no exception. But it is more in terms of making sure that their children go to the right schools, take up the right extracurricular activities, attend the right universities in Hong Kong or overseas, and generally achieve academic distinction so as to bring credit to their respective families. Most of the local mothers may be characterized as "tiger moms," to use a term coined by Amy Chua, a professor of Yale University Law School and the author of the bestselling book, *Battle Hymn of the Tiger Mother*.[5]

Universal primary and secondary school education has been achieved in Hong Kong. However, there is still a great deal of room for improvement in the educational system. Unfortunately, a short-term, self-centered, "what is in it for me" mentality prevails in Hong Kong society today.

IKEDA: I think that that disposition is perhaps not restricted to Hong Kong; it has become a major issue in Japan and around the world. Many educators with whom I have spoken expressed their concern over this matter; they are also worried about the effects of excessive individualism. I believe that this reflects the obsession with short-term economic gain that characterizes modern society.

Several years ago, I discussed university education with Jim Garrison (professor of philosophy of education at Virginia Tech in Blacksburg) and Larry Hickman (professor of philosophy at Southern Illinois University Carbondale), successive presidents of the John Dewey Society in the United States, and both expressed the same concern. According to Dr. Hickman, "Faculty should be well informed, committed to the intellectual and moral growth of their students, and, perhaps most important, willing to learn from their students as well as to teach them."[6]

Moreover, Dr. Garrison noted:

> In the past, students perceived the university as intrinsically valuable because it helped them cultivate their unique potential for personal and social growth. . . . Now, for too many, it has only exchange value; students pur-

chase it and exchange the value added for a better job, higher income, and greater social status. They confuse *having* more with *being* more. At the same time, in the last few years, there have been signs that students again want a more value-creating education. . . . [7]

One of the central purposes of education is, in my view, to overcome myopic self-centeredness.

LAU: In terms of quality, even though glowing rankings have been received by some universities in Hong Kong from some foreign consulting firms, they are in fact quite a distance from the top of the world in terms of academic excellence. It is still the case that Hong Kong students with parents who have had university-level education do not choose to enroll at Hong Kong universities—the great majority of these students go abroad. Hong Kong must try to expand, improve, and upgrade its tertiary educational sector, both qualitatively and quantitatively, in order to maintain its overall competitiveness and its relative living standard for its residents in the long run.

LANGUAGE STUDY

IKEDA: I appreciate your candor. I have also heard that even if every university in Hong Kong were at maximum enrollment, the system would still be incapable of providing every eighteen-year-old who resides there with a higher education.

CUHK was established in 1963 with the merging of three colleges. In the half century since then, together with the University of Hong Kong, CUHK has been a driving force in the advancement of higher education in Hong Kong.

I was intrigued by the results of a survey indicating that, between 1970 and 1983, more than 70 percent of CUHK students came from low-income families, while less than 5 percent were from high-income families.[8] This attests to the extent to which CUHK remains accessible to financially underprivileged students as long as they are passionate about learning, providing the opportunity for higher education to a broad spectrum of people.

LAU: At this point, you may find it interesting for me to digress and recount the story of the founding of CUHK.

Prior to 1949, Hong Kong schools were divided between Chinese-track and English- or Anglo-track, depending on the language of instruction used. The Chinese-track schools fed into mainland Chinese universities, while the Anglo-track fed into the University of Hong Kong or British universities. The students of the Chinese-track schools would enroll in mainland universities upon their graduation from senior middle schools.

However, after the establishment of the People's Republic of China in 1949, this became mostly impossible. For a while, many of these graduates went to Taiwan for their tertiary studies. And quite a few attended post-secondary colleges, such as Chung Chi College, New Asia College, and United College, established in Hong Kong by scholars and intellectuals who left the mainland in 1949.

However, the degrees granted by these colleges were not officially recognized by the Hong Kong government at the time. So the challenge was to find a way for the graduates of the Chinese-track secondary schools to pursue further studies at the tertiary level.

Initially, there was a proposal to establish a Chinese Language Division at the University of Hong Kong to accommodate these graduates. But the academic senate voted it down. After a few twists and turns, the Hong Kong government finally decided, in 1963, to establish CUHK through the amalgamation of Chung

Chi, New Asia, and United Colleges to serve this group of young people.

IKEDA: Today, CUHK is world renowned as one of Asia's premier universities. For instance, it was listed in 2008 among the top ten universities in Asia by the *Times Higher Education* magazine (affiliated with the British newspaper *The Times*).[9]

When I spoke with you on an earlier occasion, you said that the goals of CUHK are internationalization, pursuit of excellence in research, and enhancement of the quality education it provides. While we have touched on educational quality in this discussion, I would like to hear your thoughts on internationalization, particularly regarding language instruction. I understand that in Hong Kong, a growing number of schools are adding classes conducted in Putonghua, also known as Mandarin,[10] the lingua franca of modern China, in addition to Cantonese, the dialect used most prominently in Hong Kong.

LAU: Going forward, Hong Kong must try to find a uniquely useful role for itself within the Chinese nation if it is to avoid becoming just one of many Chinese cities. Hong Kong's cultural heritage, combining the Chinese and the British, the East and the West, makes it uniquely positioned to enhance understanding between China on the one hand and Western nations on the other. Even though Hong Kong is no longer a British colony, English should be just as important, if not more important, as Chinese to enable Hong Kong to maintain its position as a gateway, a bridge, connecting China and the rest of the world.

In order to fulfill its role as an intermediary, Hong Kong must at the same time enhance its links with and understanding of the mainland. And this means that the people of Hong Kong must brush up on their written Chinese (not the colloquial version of

Cantonese used in the Hong Kong tabloids) and improve their conversational ability in Putonghua. Eventually, if Hong Kong is to be competitive as a world city, everyone in Hong Kong should be proficient in both English and Putonghua, in addition to Cantonese. If Hong Kong succeeds in doing so, it can be more than a link between the East and West; it can be a link between Northeast and Southeast Asia. It can be a financial, trade, and even educational hub for the entire East Asia region. It can play a role way beyond simply being a gateway to and from mainland China.

IKEDA: Language instruction should then prove even more foundational to Hong Kong's further development.

Students from Hong Kong Soka Kindergarten, which I founded, have won awards for English and Putonghua numerous times at the Hong Kong Schools Speech Festival.[11] The fact that such contests for primary school students are popular in Hong Kong attests to the importance people there assign to language education.

While a variety of initiatives are surely being carried out in Hong Kong classrooms, what aspects of university-level language education, in your opinion, need to be reinforced?

LAU: There is one aspect that has not changed enough in academia, and that is the use of Putonghua. Due to the increase of economic interactions, including tourism, between Hong Kong and the mainland, the proficiency of the average Hong Kong resident in Putonghua has greatly improved since 1997. However, the change has been very slow at the universities—the use of Putonghua in lectures and discussion sections has not increased very much and remains below the level in the 1960s.

CUHK has always promoted the use of two languages and three dialects, meaning the Chinese and English languages and English and the two Chinese dialects—Putonghua and Cantonese. When I met the students at CUHK for the first time, before assuming the presidency of the university, I said that as far as academia is concerned, it would only be "two languages and two dialects (Putonghua and English) as Cantonese, which cannot be properly written out at all, is not a useful medium for academic exchange." I was roundly criticized for looking down on Cantonese and being politically incorrect. However, as a scholar, I stand by what I said. It is in the interests of Hong Kong tertiary educational institutions to promote the use of Putonghua on their campuses.

EXCELLENCE BEGETS EXCELLENCE

IKEDA: I'm told many students from mainland China are now also studying at CUHK.

Language education must respond to the needs of a given society. One key element in learning another language is that the learners can gain a global perspective on issues; it also enhances their ability to objectively view and compare their own culture with other cultures while affording them the opportunity for rediscovery.

Universities across Japan are emphasizing language studies, and they are doing this through programs unique to each school. The economics faculty of Soka University, for example, has an international program in which the students study economics in English. Students have taken to the program, and it is now attracting the attention of many in the field of education.

In recognition of our ongoing efforts, the Japanese Ministry of Education, Culture, Sports, Science, and Technology announced that Soka University has been chosen as a partner institution in the Project for Promotion of Global Human Resource Development[12] in 2012 and the Top Global University Project in 2014.[13] The freshmen who enrolled starting in April 2014 can choose to learn foreign languages from the sixteen language programs our school now offers. Meanwhile, plans are underway to institute

English-language instruction in every faculty, including the Faculty of Nursing, which was dedicated in April 2013. In the spring of 2014, moreover, our school will be launching its new Faculty of International Liberal Arts, in which students must spend a full year studying abroad starting in the second semester of their freshman year. Upon their return, every class in their major will be conducted in English.

A core concern for universities worldwide is to provide students with a broad range of both academic and specialized knowledge, as well as a proficient command of foreign languages, so that they are capable of excelling in an era of globalization.

What steps is CUHK taking to pursue excellence in research, the third of the three goals of the university?

LAU: With the reversion of Hong Kong to Chinese sovereignty and the continuing economic and social progress of China, CUHK faces competition not only from universities in Hong Kong but also from universities on the mainland. I believe CUHK has the potential to become the best university in China—that is, in Greater China, including not only Hong Kong and the mainland, but also Macau and Taiwan.

How can CUHK maintain its top rank among Chinese universities? In the long run, the university can compete only through excellence—excellence in research, with which it can build and sustain its academic reputation, helping attract the best young faculty members and graduate students; and excellence in undergraduate education, enabling it to attract the best undergraduate students, who would then go on to become its best alumni. Being able to retain and recruit the best teachers, teachers with distinguished research achievements and international academic reputations, will help attract the best graduate and undergraduate students; having the best students will in turn attract the best teachers.

Thus, excellence begets excellence. It is a self-perpetuating, virtuous cycle, once it gets started. That is why universities such as Cambridge, Oxford, Harvard, and Yale have been, are, and will remain on top.

IKEDA: I have fond memories of my visits to Cambridge, Oxford, and Harvard. They are unquestionably sublime bastions of wisdom and knowledge, imparting a tangible sense that academic tradition is synonymous with strength.

For every university, teaching and research may be likened to two wheels on an axle. Furthermore, I agree with your observation that an institution's excellence in research and undergraduate instruction will determine its future. I am equally cognizant that CUHK is more than capable of emerging as the finest university in all of Greater China.

In January 1992, I had the privilege of delivering a lecture, "Traditional Chinese Humanism Will Shine in the New Century," at CUHK, whose achievements thus far have been nothing short of remarkable. In the lecture, I referred to your university motto, *bo wen yue li:* "to broaden one's intellectual horizons; to keep within the bounds of propriety," which is derived from the *Analects of Confucius.* This inspires students to engage others with moral integrity while excelling not only in their chosen disciplines but as human beings. I also expressed my belief that it is vital to continuously evaluate and reaffirm the value and worth of a philosophy through its application in daily life.

This was my concluding thought:

> In these troubled times when people aspire to create an epoch in which humanism assumes center stage, I cannot help but believe that a revival of the sublime spiritual tradition of China will contribute greatly to the realization of a century of humanity.

I am therefore convinced that the Chinese University of Hong Kong will prove invaluable in this task, and just like the Chinese phoenix portrayed in your school emblem, impel the winds of hope throughout Asia and the world in the twenty-first century.[14]

I believe this to be true now more than ever and look forward to forging even stronger bonds of friendship with you and your university, and to making many new discoveries along the way.

CONVERSATION THREE

Successful Higher Education

IKEDA: One of life's greatest joys is encountering opportunities for further intellectual discovery. Such enlightening experiences are borne out of dialogue with insightful and intelligent minds, driving one's never-ending quest for self-development. This is why I thoroughly enjoy taking part in this discourse and watching how it unfolds.

I once had the opportunity to meet with Harvard University President Neil Rudenstine (in September 1991 at Harvard). When I asked him about the role of his institution in the world, he said:

> Harvard is an international university. It is visited by students and academic staff from countries around the world, including Japan, and Harvard, too, has ventured into other countries. Our campus is in the United States, but its influence extends to the entire world. Although Harvard is an American educational institution, it embraces and accepts students from all over the world and then, when they graduate, sends them back out into the world. So, as it were, Harvard creates the world in and of itself. It strives to look at the world from an all-round perspective.

> Great scholars are those who, wherever they may be
> in this complicated world, can feel as if they are living in
> their own country.[1]

In the future, excellence and global perspective in research are certain to become increasingly paramount. What do you see as some of the core areas that a university must address to flourish in the years ahead?

LAU: And what about a university that is not there yet? That has yet to excel? How can such a university achieve excellence?

In the twentieth century, three universities in the United States have achieved world-class status, starting from relatively modest initial academic standings. They are the Massachusetts Institute of Technology, Stanford University, and the University of Southern California. Coincidentally, all three are private, nonprofit universities.

MIT took advantage of its proximity to Harvard University to recruit up-and-coming faculty members from Harvard, people whom Harvard was either unable or unwilling to retain. An example was the late Professor Paul A. Samuelson, Nobel laureate in economic sciences, who was quickly offered a position at MIT when Harvard decided not to give him tenure. He went on to build the Department of Economics at MIT to be one of the best in the United States.

Between World War I and World War II, MIT also recruited worldwide, bringing many distinguished scholars from Europe to America. By the end of World War II, the quality of the faculty at MIT was sufficient to put it on a par with its neighbor, Harvard University, both in Cambridge, Massachusetts.

In the mid-1950s, Stanford University was fortunate to have a president, J. E. Wallace Sterling, and a provost, Frederick Terman, who worked together to turn Stanford into a world-class educational and research institution in less than two decades. Dr. Sterling managed to attract many large donations to Stanford with which to establish chaired professorships, build new academic buildings, and finance various other activities. Dr. Terman focused on the recruitment of the top teachers and researchers from around the world. He established and promoted the Stanford Industrial Park and persuaded many research-based industries to locate at Stanford.

The two made use of the 9,000-acre Stanford campus to develop residential areas for faculty members. They also pioneered the establishment of overseas campuses—in France, Germany, and Italy—to help attract the best undergraduate students. The rest, as they say, is history. Stanford University today is generally regarded as one of the world's top-ranked, comprehensive research universities.

IKEDA: Yes, I've been informed at some length about how the recruitment of outstanding researchers and faculty members from around the world has been a major force in propelling Stanford, at which you not only studied but also successfully taught for many years. I'm also proud to note that a number of Soka University of America alumni have pursued their postgraduate studies at Stanford and similar universities with world-class faculties such as Harvard, Cambridge, and the University of California, Berkeley, where you also once studied.

Which brings us to the challenge faced by universities in general: How do they manage to harmonize the different demands of research and education and maximize the synergy of these two pillars of higher learning? This has been an oft-discussed issue.

The German philosopher Karl Jaspers described the relationship between university research and teaching in *The Idea of the*

University, which he published just after the unconditional sur-
render of Nazi Germany:

> Teaching vitally needs the substance which only research
> can give it. Hence the combination of research and teach-
> ing is the lofty and inalienable basic principle of the uni-
> versity. . . . Ideally the best research worker is also the best
> and only teacher.[2]

Jaspers thought that because the university is a place of higher
learning that deals with what could be called "living scholarship,"
excellent teachers must concurrently be excellent researchers. He
maintained that research and teaching were inseparable, and that
the superb union of the two was essential in creating an outstanding university in the truest sense. I believe this to be a valid point.
Indeed, achieving this union can be described as a major challenge for all universities today.

LAU: USC recruited Dr. Steven B. Sample to be its tenth president
in 1991. Dr. Sample served as president for twenty years, until
2010, and he completely transformed USC during his tenure. He
expanded and upgraded USC's School of Engineering, particularly
in electrical and electronic engineering, computer science, and
communication, fields in which there is considerable industrial
strength in Southern California. He managed to attract many
large donations to USC from private individuals and corporations.

He cleaned up the impoverished neighborhood around the USC
campus by offering financial and other incentives for the homeowners and residents there to improve their dwellings and the
surrounding environment. The result is that everyone, including
faculty members and students, can all feel safer and more secure,
and the campus has become a place in which professors and students can focus their attention and energy on scholarly activities.

He capitalized on USC's proximity to Hollywood to develop its strengths in the field of media, including film, journalism, and mass communication. He also recruited the best faculty members to come to USC. And he made USC the university with the largest number of undergraduate students from foreign countries. Today, USC is a top-ranked university in the United States and in the world.

The experiences of MIT, Stanford, and USC show that it is entirely possible for a university to achieve world-class standards in a couple decades. There are many different factors—leadership, people, resources, etc.—that make such an achievement possible, but excellence in the quality of the research output of its faculty members is an absolutely essential ingredient.

WHOLE-PERSON EDUCATION

IKEDA: Soka University of Japan has exchange programs with USC, including a short-term study-abroad program every fall. Preparations are also underway for USC to accept students from the Faculty of International Liberal Arts.

In February 1990, I visited the USC Fisher Museum of Art. The museum was scheduled to hold the exhibition *Land of Gentle Smiles: Special Exhibition of Photographs by His Majesty King Bhumibol Adulyadej of Thailand* from March that year. As the founder of the Tokyo Fuji Art Museum, which was cosponsoring the exhibition, I went to pay my respects to the museum's director, Selma Holo.

This exhibition came about as a result of a meeting I was granted with His Majesty, whose interest in and knowledge of the arts and culture are profound. I took that opportunity to personally secure his blessing and support. In addition to the United States, the exhibition was also held in Tokyo and the United Kingdom. Given this start of our history with USC, I am delighted to see that educational exchange between Soka University of Japan and USC has continued to move steadily forward.

You stressed the importance of a university assembling an outstanding faculty. This was one of our most difficult challenges when establishing Soka University in 1971—to assemble the best possible faculty. At the time, leftists and rightists in Japan were locked in a meaningless ideological struggle. University campuses, which were marred by constant clashes between student demonstrators and riot police, were fraught with unrest and uncertainty. I was thus determined to find a new way forward for education.

Soka University was founded out of the desire to foster bright young people who will build a new age of peace and culture, to be an institution dedicated to educating a seamless procession of capable individuals working for our world's betterment. As we strove to share this dream to the best of our abilities, many eminent, outstanding teachers and scholars were moved by the purity of our purpose and joined our faculty.

Forty-three years have passed since then, and in April 2013, Yoshihisa Baba became the first Soka University graduate to be appointed university president. I remain profoundly grateful to every member of the faculty who supported our university in its early days.

Lau: I congratulate you on the appointment of a new university president.

As I mentioned previously, good students tend to attract good teachers, and good teachers in turn tend to attract good students. Having the best teachers and having the best students reinforce each other. CUHK aspires to be a research-based university, an international university, and a university that emphasizes whole-person education, making use of its unique college system. It is hoped that the graduates of the university will be endowed not only with knowledge and reason but also commitment to public service, responsibility and compassion, and a global perspective.

IKEDA: Yes, the kind of all-around education that CUHK is providing has even greater importance today. What, then, do you regard as the attributes of a good teacher?

LAU: The ideal qualities of a teacher are not that different from those of a student, which should include intellectual curiosity and intellectual honesty. They should be accomplished researchers in their respective fields. But a good teacher must also try to customize or personalize his or her teaching to the student or students— there is no one size that fits all. The teacher should also teach and lead by personal example and should always put the long-term interests of the students first.

Patience is yet another desirable attribute of a good teacher. A good teacher teaches in a way that is easy to understand, that arouses intellectual interest and curiosity, and that makes the students think for themselves. Both Socrates and Confucius taught through dialogues with their students, by using the question-and-answer method, although each in his own way.

IKEDA: Every point you raise is quite convincing. I once shared with our faculty members these words from French philosopher Jean-Jacques Rousseau's treatise on education, *Emile*:

> There are callings so noble that one cannot follow them
> for money without proving oneself unworthy of following
> them. . . . [S]uch is that of the teacher.[3]

I cannot stress enough how important an educator is in fostering human beings, which I believe to be a sacred task. The student who encounters a teacher of superior learning and character, a teacher who compassionately interacts with those in his or her care with firm belief in their potential, is indeed blessed. And I agree that dialogue is a crucial form of interactive learning for life in general.

As I mentioned earlier, one-on-one dialogue was the method through which I studied with my mentor in my twenties. He tutored me every Sunday at first, but because that was not enough, we started to meet every morning before the workday began. Aside from being an elementary school teacher, he was a mathematical genius, and his *Suirishiki shido sanjutsu* (A Deductive Guide to Arithmetic), which was published before the war, was a bestseller. He was equally well versed in a vast range of subjects.

At our private lessons, he would not allow me to take notes, saying that I should engrave in my heart what he imparted. The training I received from him was quite strict, but to this day, I remain profoundly grateful for the opportunity to learn at "Toda University." I do not say this because Mr. Toda was my mentor but because I have never met a person who excelled in every leadership skill as he did.

BORN IN TURBULENT TIMES

IKEDA: Incidentally, your name *Zunyi* comes from the town in Guizhou Province of southwestern China where you were born, doesn't it? You were born on December 12, 1944, the year before the fighting ended that had marred China for more than a decade since the Manchurian Incident.[4] I understand that you were born while your parents were fleeing from Guilin to Chongqing, in the face of a Japanese military offensive. I can only imagine how painful and difficult that journey must have been for your parents and other members of your family.

I also understand that Yu Youren named you. He was a comrade and close friend of Sun Yat-sen, who founded China's first republic, and, as I mentioned earlier (see Conversation One), not only a revolutionary activist but also an eminent educator and artist.

LAU: As you said, I was born toward the end of World War II, in the town of Zunyi in Guizhou Province. My parents, Liu Shai-Tat and Yu Chi-Hing, lived in Hong Kong before the Japanese invasion and occupation of Hong Kong in 1941. However, afterward, my parents moved back to the city of Guilin, in Guangxi Province, where my late paternal grandfather, Liu Hou-Wu, served as the representative of the Control Yuan[5] for the Guangdong and Guangxi Provinces, working under my maternal grandfather, Yu Youren, who was then the president of the Control Yuan.

Toward the end of 1944, the Japanese military offensive threatened Guilin, and my family had to flee the city for Chongqing, the wartime capital. I was born en route, in Zunyi. I was born in the Magistrate's Courthouse, which apparently was also the location for holding imperial examinations for the region in the Qing dynasty. Afterward, my grandfather named me after the town in which I was born.

IKEDA: The Japanese invasion of China inflicted unspeakable hardship and suffering on the Chinese. As a Japanese citizen, I must express my heartfelt contrition for those tragic times.

The year of your birth, 1944, was the year that my fourth-oldest brother was drafted. We said our goodbyes to him at Shinagawa Station in Tokyo as he was taken away in a military train.

There were eight children in my family, of which I was the fifth son. I was born in what is now Ota Ward in Tokyo. Our family made a living cultivating and processing *nori* (edible seaweed). The business flourished for a time, but my father was stricken with crippling rheumatism that left him bedridden. From that time, our family business quickly began to unravel. To make matters worse, my four older brothers were all drafted to fight in the war.

I contracted tuberculosis in my mid-teens, but I worked at a factory to help support our family. My mother had to shoulder a heavy burden, but she never uttered a single complaint. It's always the ordinary people who suffer in war.

My eldest brother, upon returning home on furlough from the Chinese front, spoke to me of his outrage at the invading Japanese forces. "There's nothing glorious about war," he insisted. "The Japanese army is imperious. I pity the people of China." Later, he died in the fighting in Burma. We only learned of his death nearly two years after the war's end. My parents were overwhelmed with grief; I still remember the sight of my brave mother's trembling shoulders as she wept, her back turned to me.

Immediately after that tragic news, I first encountered Mr. Toda, who later became the second president of the Soka Gakkai, at a discussion meeting held in Kamata, Ota Ward, to which a friend invited me. Mr. Toda was lecturing on "On Establishing the Correct Teaching for the Peace of the Land," a treatise by Nichiren, a Buddhist thinker and reformer in Japan.[6] Toda's heartfelt insistence that he wanted to eliminate all suffering and misery from the face of the Earth shook my young being to the core. As I mentioned earlier, I learned of Mr. Toda's two-year incarceration for opposing the policies of Japan's militarist government, and I decided to dedicate my life to working for peace together with him as my lifelong mentor.

I have a deep connection with Ota, for I was not only born there but met my mentor there.

What kind of place was Zunyi, your birthplace?

FANATICAL NATIONALISM

LAU: The city of Zunyi has a long history, dating back to the Shang dynasty. It adopted its current name in the Tang dynasty, probably from a phrase in the *Book of History*: "*wu pian wu po / zun wang zhi yi*" (honoring the duty of the lord without bias or imbalance). There is also a gate in the Imperial Palace in the Forbidden City in Beijing that is named Zunyimen, which I believe probably also has the same origin as the name of the city.

By pure coincidence, Zunyi is the location of the pivotal conference of the Politburo of the Chinese Communist Party, held midway on the Long March in January 1935, at which Chairman Mao Zedong finally assumed control of the party. This is known as the Zunyi Conference in the Chinese history books, although the conference itself was shrouded in secrecy until 1956. Today, the site where the Zunyi Conference was held has become a place of pilgrimage for the party faithful.

IKEDA: Having learned how the city came to be named Zunyi, I can see why Yu chose the namesake for you.

I'm also curious how many siblings you have.

LAU: I have an elder brother, Eddy Tai-Kwan, who was born in Guilin in 1942, and a younger brother, Taiching, who was born in Chongqing in early 1946. A still younger brother, John Tai-Kong, was born in Hong Kong in early 1947, and my youngest brother, Patrick Yan-Shui, was born in 1949.

There were five sons in my family. My parents really wanted a daughter. In fact, their first-born child was a daughter, but she died before Eddy was born, a sister whom I never knew.

IKEDA: Your parents must have been deeply saddened by her death. No doubt their daughter remained in their thoughts throughout their lives.

Your family returned to Hong Kong after the war, then?

LAU: After World War II, some time in 1946, my parents moved back to Hong Kong from Chongqing, and we lived at 7 Garden

Terrace, on the second floor of a three-story house. Our down-stairs neighbor was Dr. Li Sung, the doctor who had delivered me in Zunyi in late 1944.

Hong Kong was a city of only two million people when I grew up there. There were very few high-rise buildings. Around us, at the time, was plenty of unimproved land in the wild, where my brothers and I often went out and played soccer and other games. We would pick stones and rocks that glittered in the sun because we thought they were valuable. (Of course, they were not.)

By the late 1940s and early 1950s, there were very few signs left of the Japanese occupation (from late 1941 to mid-1945). Our family had moved back to mainland China after the Japanese army entered Hong Kong and did not have to live through the Japanese military occupation. But many who did still remembered the hardships and continued to feel a great deal of hatred for the Japanese at that time. And occasionally, old bank notes issued by the Japanese military government would appear, reminding people once again of the harshness of the occupation period.

The focus of my parents' circle of friends was no longer on the conflict between China and Japan but the conflict between the nationalists and the communists. Both my paternal grandfather and father were members of the Kuomintang (Nationalist) Party and they were very much anti-communist. Grandfather Yu had gone to Taiwan to join the Nationalist Government in the meantime.

During the period of 1948–49, many people came to Hong Kong as refugees. I remember we had house guests almost every day. Some stayed a couple days. Some stayed for weeks. A few would stay for months. Eventually, they all left. I did not realize then why they were in our home, but now I know that they were all refugees of the Chinese Civil War.

IKEDA: The Japanese forces invaded the Kowloon Peninsula (part of Hong Kong) in December 1941, at roughly the same time they attacked Pearl Harbor in Hawaii.

Some have described the twentieth century as a century of war and violence driven by ideological extremism and fanatical nationalism. I strongly feel that we must never forget the bitter lessons of history under militarism and the atrocities perpetrated as a result. I vigorously oppose the violence perpetrated under ultra-nationalism, which treats people as simply a means to an end—and I will fight against any move toward its reemergence for as long as I live.

Moving on, you remained in Hong Kong, which was then undergoing remarkable growth, until leaving to study in the United States.

HONG KONG AS FINANCIAL CENTER

LAU: Around this time, Henry Y. T. Fok, the entrepreneur and philanthropist, introduced a simple yet critical innovation to the Hong Kong real estate market. Heretofore, it had not been possible for a building to have subdivided ownership—it had to be wholly owned by a single individual or entity. This rule severely reduced the demand for new buildings because there would be few potential purchasers who could afford an entire building, even with leverage through bank loans. With little demand, there would be little supply. Thus, few new buildings were built, and those that were built were of limited size (so as to maintain affordability for the few who could purchase entire buildings). Mr. Fok basically figured out the legal arrangements for subdivided, or condominium, ownership of a building, making it possible to sell individual floors or individual units on the same floor to different individuals or entities.

Thus, all of a sudden, many people who had been renters became eligible buyers and owners of their residential units. This innovation started a housing boom in Hong Kong that lasted a couple decades, briefly interrupted by the riots of 1966 and 1967.[7]

IKEDA: That was around the time we entered the age of jets and jumbo aircraft, and the aviation industry increased the exchange of people and goods. Hong Kong became an important center of air transportation in Asia.

Listening to your recollections has started to bring back many fond memories of Hong Kong since my first visit in 1961. As I have said numerous times before, I adore the city of Hong Kong. I have walked its streets and engaged in lively conversations and exchanges with many residents. Of course, it is attractive as a "fragrant harbor"—the meaning of *Hong Kong*—where East meets West, but more than anything I have, again, always been struck by the people's tremendous vitality. Over the past several decades, Hong Kong has also emerged as a major financial center of the world, a remarkable feat that began in the previous century and continues to this day.

As with Shanghai, a number of Chinese cities have become important gateways to the world after experiencing dramatic economic growth after China's "Reform and Opening Up" process[8] under Deng Xiaoping. How do you see Hong Kong's economic relationship with mainland China and with East Asia changing? What is your long-term outlook on Hong Kong? I know you touched on this earlier, but I'd be grateful if you would provide us with further details.

LAU: As you suggest, Hong Kong faces challenges as China becomes more and more open and more closely integrated with the rest of the world. Hong Kong currently has the advantages of free capital mobility and a fully convertible currency. However, these advantages may disappear by 2020.

Shanghai has the advantages of being more centrally located, a much larger economy as well as population, and a more highly educated labor force. (Shanghai has many more tertiary educational institutions and research institutes than Hong Kong.) The recently announced establishment of the China (Shanghai) Pilot Free Trade Zone is an attempt on the part of Shanghai to accelerate its integration into the world economy. We should bear in mind that before 1949, Shanghai was much more prosperous and internationalized than Hong Kong.

Rather than competing with Shanghai head to head, what Hong Kong should do is to collaborate and cooperate with Shanghai as much as it can and agree with Shanghai on a suitable division of labor. The Chinese economy is large enough to have two or even more international financial centers.

The natural economic hinterland for Shanghai is the Yangzi River Delta region and the natural economic hinterland for Hong Kong is the Pearl River Delta region. Hong Kong's immediate neighbor, Guangdong Province, has a population of almost 100 million. Together with Shenzhen, Hong Kong, and Macau, the total population exceeds 110 million—larger than that of Germany and almost equal to that of Japan. Guangdong, Shenzhen, Hong Kong, and Macau combined have a total GDP of more than $1.2 trillion and a per capita GDP of more than $11,000. In addition, despite the recent slowdown in the Chinese economy, this region is still growing, albeit not as rapidly as before. Hong Kong can certainly continue to prosper by serving as the financial center of this combined region.

Another role that Hong Kong can play, taking advantage of the rapidly growing demand for insurance and reinsurance of all kinds and the plentiful supply of risk capital in the region, is to try to establish itself as the insurance/reinsurance center for East Asia, supplanting London and Zurich, the existing reinsurance centers of the world. The fact that there is a long tradition of the rule of law in Hong Kong is an additional advantage—enterprises and individuals who purchase insurance generally want to be paid off as soon as possible should adverse events occur and not spend years in inconclusive litigation.

Still another possibility is for Hong Kong to try to develop a pan-East Asia securities exchange on which the stocks and bonds of all major East Asian firms and the bonds of all East Asian governments can be listed and traded. For example, on this securities exchange, it should be possible to purchase shares in Toyota, Samsung, Taiwan Semiconductor Manufacturing Corporation, San Miguel, HSBC, Singapore Airlines, Siam Cement, Indo Foods, etc. Thus, investors around the world interested in East Asia could simply base themselves in Hong Kong and have easy access to all the shares of these best companies of East Asia, all in one single currency, without having to worry about exchange rate changes and capital controls.

Finally, Hong Kong and Shanghai can cross-list the shares of their best companies. By so doing, the liquidity of these shares will increase and the investor pool will be enlarged, benefitting the listed companies, the investors, and both Hong Kong and Shanghai.

IKEDA: Thank you for answering my question in such a clear, succinct manner. Your reply not only takes into account the changing times but also represents a vision of the future based on a broad, insightful perspective.

The world will be following Hong Kong closely as this gateway city and member of China's "extended family" pursues further development. I am confident that Hong Kong remains strategically positioned for growth, given its geographic advantage as a hub for intra-Asian commerce and China's nearby and immense material and human resources.

Above all, the Hong Kong people are blessed with broad-mindedness and a worldview quite cosmopolitan; they are also flush with drive and vigor. Indeed, every time Hong Kong has encountered difficulties over the years, it has succeeded in prevailing over them.

In 1997, I presented a poem to my Hong Kong friends just before the reversion. Allow me to introduce several stanzas here:

> Let us now set forth,
> my beloved friends of Hong Kong!
> A brand new stage
> awaits your arrival
> with open arms.
>
> The history of Hong Kong
> is an exquisite painted scroll
> heralding the triumph of ordinary people,
> a dramatic tale of indomitable lives
> unbowed before every hardship.
>
> Despite history's kaleidoscopic turns and twists,
> the people of Hong Kong have never succumbed!
> Lauded for their abounding fight and mettle,
> they have boldly led to the very end
> lives as stout and hardy
> as shoots breaking through the hinterland.
>
> Never looking back on what once was,
> you stand firmly on reality's great earth
> with gazes fixed on the future.
> Brows bright with sweat, you toil on,
> sparing no effort
> in all honestness.
>
> You have coped with change
> by being flexible yet determined,

a most enterprising spirit
always thinking, constantly tinkering.
Absorbing the winds of the world,
your thirst for learning remains unsated.

Hong Kong has thus been resurrected,
a phoenix rising from dread and uncertainty
to soar the open skies of the century,
a city that has earned its miraculous prosperity
as a mighty gateway to the world.

Therein lies proof
of the insuperable spirit of its people,
a proud legacy symbolizing Hong Kong's very soul.[9]

I, for one, believe Hong Kong will continue to flourish as a crossroads at which East and West meet in harmony and as a harbor for peace. I hold the highest expectations for Hong Kong's boundless energy and potential, confident that it will serve as a beacon to transmit to the world new cultural values in the twenty-first century.

The Joy of Learning

IKEDA: In whatever era or land, young people have always represented hope for the future. My hope is that they reach for the highest ideals and strive to build a better society, prevailing over every challenge and difficulty with youthful vigor and passion. It is the mission and hallmark of youth to open the doors to a new age. And the true spirit of every educator lies in cherishing and respecting young people, fostering them into individuals even more capable than the educators themselves.

In this conversation, to encourage our young readers as they tackle new challenges and innovations, would you discuss your childhood and youth, as well as the education and other life lessons your parents provided as you were growing up? Where did your parents originally come from?

LAU: My father grew up in Chaoyang Xian, a district near Shantou, Guangdong. He attended primary school in Guangzhou (Canton), secondary school in Shanghai, and then Chuo University in Tokyo in the 1930s, but I believe he did not graduate and had to return to China along with other Chinese students who were in Japan at the time.

My father went to Taiwan for business quite early, perhaps in 1947, and was also engaged in business in Shanghai. He was the manager of Taiwan Livestock Industry Co., Ltd.

IKEDA: My mentor also studied at Chuo University. That makes him and your father fellow alumni.

Earlier, we discussed Yu Youren's visit to Japan (see Conversation One). I recall you saying that your family has strong ties to Japan.

LAU: My grandfather Yu Youren visited Japan in 1906 and, as you mentioned previously, he met Dr. Sun Yat-sen, the founder of the Republic of China, for the first time there. He also joined the Tung-Meng Hui, a revolutionary society that was the precursor of the Kuomintang. My father attended Chuo University in Japan and had many friends there.

My mother grew up in Sanyuan Xian, a district near Xian, the ancient capital of China. My parents were married in Hong Kong in the late 1930s. My mother worked at the Central Trust of China until my brothers and I came along. She had to take care of all five of us, often by herself, because my father was managing a business in Taiwan. My mother was a kind and gentle soul. I remember she loved flowers. She would always have fresh flowers at our home: ginger, gladiolus, and so forth. Her tastes were simple yet elegant. My mother was frugal but not stingy.

IKEDA: Her wise, loving nature comes through clearly in your description. Could you share some of the lessons she imparted that remain with you?

LAU: One episode that I still remember vividly was her telling me that if I were the last person to leave a room, I must remember to switch off the lights. It is something that I still do regularly.

She was strict but fair. She insisted on the best manners both at home as well as outside. Above all, she was always concerned with our education. She wanted us to have the best opportunities.

That was the primary reason that Eddy, my elder brother, and I were left in Hong Kong to complete our schooling. As our parents and our younger siblings moved to Taiwan in 1953, Eddy and I remained in Hong Kong with our maternal grandmother so that we could continue to attend St. Paul's Co-educational College.

From that time on, I saw my parents only sparingly, when they visited us or when we went to Taiwan for vacations. I was, of course, quite envious of my classmates, who had many opportunities to spend time with their parents. Both Eddy and I were very happy and excited when one or both of our parents visited Hong Kong. They would take us shopping and buy us things that we had been needing for months.

IKEDA: Your mother's lesson to switch off the lights when you leave the room, a small thing though it may seem, and her seeing to it that you and your brothers acquired both good sense and good manners reinforce my appreciation for the importance of parental education. These seemingly small points are actually very important as the bases for us to acquire the right attitudes and sound wisdom to lead our lives.

I also believe that your experience living apart from your parents to pursue your studies will encourage the Soka Junior and Senior High Schools students, particularly those living in dormitories or other boarding arrangements. These students know first-hand the difficulty of living apart from their parents. It is clear, however, that this experience also fosters independence and self-reliance, as we have seen from the many capable individuals who came out of Japan's former system of secondary schools, which, like Britain's, often included dormitory living.

I am confident that many outstanding leaders will emerge from the Soka Junior and Senior High Schools.

If I might ask another question, with your limited opportunities to be with your parents, what part did your teachers play in your life during your elementary and junior high school years?

THE CAPACITY TO ACHIEVE HAPPINESS

LAU: During my formative years, several individuals, in addition to my family, had a profound influence on me. First and foremost was Dr. B. M. Kotewall, the principal of St. Paul's Co-educational College. Dr. Kotewall was never married and dedicated her whole life to the success of St. Paul's, and whatever success St. Paul's has had is due in large measure to her. Dr. Kotewall had very high standards for both academic performance and personal behavior.

I was, honestly speaking, quite mischievous when I was in secondary school. For example, one time after class, I rearranged all the desks in the classroom, so that my classmates would all miss their possessions that they kept in their own desks. I was sent to see the principal not infrequently. However, Dr. Kotewall did not think I was incorrigible and gave me many opportunities to redeem myself.

Dr. Kotewall was also a devout Christian, and she taught biblical studies. She also ran a small bible study group, and I was fortunate to become a member. She encouraged me to undertake many extracurricular activities. For example, I became the founding editor of *The Bunsen Burner*, a newspaper for the school, and, with her active support, I helped merge the Boy Scout troop of St. Paul's with that of St. John's Cathedral, creating the first racially integrated Boy Scout troop in Hong Kong.

Dr. Kotewall taught me by her words and deeds how to be an honorable, responsible person and how to maintain strict standards and compassion at the same time. We kept in touch, long after she retired and I began my teaching career in the United States.

IKEDA: I can see that she was a woman of character who devoted her life to education. Maintaining strict standards and compassion at the same time is, it seems, an apt description of Dr. Kotewall's life.

The student who encounters a good teacher will find that his or her talents will sprout and flower in a significant manner. Above all, a good teacher will impart to students the joy of learning.

Makiguchi, founder of Soka (value-creating) education, also maintained that the essential role of teachers in education is to facilitate and provide guidance and support in a child's learning process. In more specific terms, this is a process requiring the student to actively take on challenges on their own initiative.

Moreover, Makiguchi, convinced that fulfillment is to be found in the act of creating value, maintained that the goal of education is to help all children acquire the capacity to achieve happiness. This requires educators to engage each child as an individual deserving respect with an unassailable belief in their potential.

Dr. Kotewall, too, seems to have believed in the potential of each of her students, encouraged them with great patience, and lovingly fostered them. To me, the fact that she continued, even after her retirement, to be concerned about your progress and to enjoy hearing about your life in the United States makes her a model educator in the sacred task of education.

LAU: The second person was Mrs. Sandra Tao, my seventh grade (first year of secondary school) teacher, who taught me the importance of humility—that by being humble, one could listen to and learn from other people and hence would be more likely to succeed.

The third person was Marguerite Kennedy, my history teacher

during the last two or three years of secondary school. She taught me the usefulness of learning from history. She also taught me to look at the big picture, look at the long-term continental and worldwide trends, and look at the underlying forces rather than the superficial reasons for different events. I learned a great deal from her.

IKEDA: You were blessed with many fine teachers.

Humility, learning from others and from history, seeing things in terms of the big picture and the long-term perspective, viewing the essential over the transient—these qualities represent a living humanistic education and are all essential life lessons. As to how one should look at history, I am reminded that my mentor often said that we should study to foster a historical perspective. He stressed that instead of focusing on the rise and fall of the mighty, we need to view history from the standpoint of the people. The truth as ostensibly recorded in history, Toda underscored, was not necessarily synonymous with the truth.

While society has undergone great changes since the time you and I spent as youth, what are some of your hopes for the young people who must shoulder the future of Hong Kong and China?

LAU: I hope that they would all become less self-centered, more patient, and more long-term oriented, like their parents' generation; that they would develop a better work ethic and more professionalism, no matter what they do. There is too much of an entitlement culture and too much emphasis on instant gratification. Neither is desirable, nor possible and sustainable in the long run. Our basic system of values needs to be rebuilt, so that it is less materialistic or money-oriented, perhaps with the support of religions.

"Serve the People" used to be a common slogan on the mainland. It has now been half-jokingly corrupted into "Serve the People's Currency." It is unfortunately true that mainland China has become in many ways too profit-oriented and too capitalistic.

In Hong Kong, in part because of its long history as a British colony, there is still not enough knowledge of Chinese national history and too little sense of a shared Chinese nationhood. There is also insufficient commitment on the part of most of the people to work for the common good. It is very much every person for himself or herself. I hope that all of this will change in the future. However, we cannot expect a change overnight. It will have to occur gradually.

In closing, if I may borrow from John F. Kennedy's inaugural speech, I urge the young people in Hong Kong, mainland China, and Japan, to "Ask not what your country can do for you—ask what you can do for your country."[1] I do not mean to ask them to be nationalistic but instead to consider it a duty and an honor to serve their own respective societies.

CREATING A NEW SELF

IKEDA: Which is why we need to learn from every experience in our youth and make it the sustenance for our mental and spiritual growth.

Reading, especially, is a feast for the mind and a lifelong treasure—a fact that many have experienced and can readily verify. While it has been lamented that the number of young people who read books has steadily declined as such media as television and the Internet grow in popularity, people in Japan are reaffirming the importance of our print culture.

Which books did you enjoy as a young man?

LAU: In my youth, I read all of the major Chinese classic novels such as *Travels to the West, The Romance of the Three Kingdoms, The Water Margin,* and *The Dream of the Red Chamber,* but I must confess that I never really enjoyed reading *The Dream of the Red Chamber*, perhaps because I was too young then to understand and appreciate love stories. I also read all of the quasi-historical novels (*Investiture of the Gods, History of the States of Eastern Zhou, History of the States of Later Eastern Zhou, The Complete Novel of the Tang Dynasty*, etc.) from the Zhou dynasty down to the Qing dynasty. I also read the stories of the impartial and wise judge Bao Zheng in *The Seven Heroes and Five Gallants*, as well as *The Scholars*.

In secondary school, I began to read Chinese martial arts novels written by Louis Cha, also known as Jin Yong, whom you know well, beginning with *The Book and the Sword, Sword Stained with Royal Blood*, and *The Legend of the Condor Heroes*; and by Liang Yusheng, beginning with *Longhu dou jinghua* (The Dragon Fights the Tiger) and *Qijan xia tianshan* (Seven Swords of Mount Heaven). As Jin Yong's martial arts novels were often serialized in newspapers in Hong Kong, even when I was a student in the United States, I would ask my friends in Hong Kong to clip the newspaper every day and mail Jin Yong's section to me.

IKEDA: As they say, wherever there are Chinese people, you will find Jin Yong novels. Since his novels have been translated into Japanese now, many of my Japanese friends are also fans of the Chinese writer's works.

On a number of occasions, I have had the privilege of meeting with Jin Yong. I have fond memories of our collaboration on *Compassionate Light in Asia*, a dialogue we engaged in—which was serialized by monthly magazines in both Hong Kong and Japan— as we watched history in the making around the time of Hong Kong's reversion.

In our dialogue, we discussed in depth such seminal works of Chinese literature as *The Romance of the Three Kingdoms* and *The Water Margin*; great Chinese writers such as Lu Xun and Ba

Jin; the works of the French writer Victor Hugo; and *The Count of Monte Cristo* by the French author Alexandre Dumas. We discussed many other subjects as well, engaging in a frank exchange of ideas on such topics as the future of Hong Kong and promoting further exchange between Hong Kong and Japan.

I read most of this outstanding literature with Toda and learned a great deal about leadership, life, and human nature. When we used the historical novel *The Water Margin* as a textbook, for example, my mentor said he'd like to read it as a thrilling commentary on social reform. By saying so, he was underscoring the importance of grasping the novel's underlying thinking and beliefs that the author wanted to express.

Toda further impressed on me the need to read literary masterpieces in a reflective manner to heighten my ability to observe and understand people in general. Saying that the times themselves are a powerful force to be reckoned with, he taught that a person could not be properly understood unless we understood the historical context in which the person lived. In short, my mentor was striving to foster young leaders who would shoulder the future and serve in advancing ordinary people's happiness.

I once asked an American friend [Dr. Victoria B. Cass, wife of Stephen Dunham, chair of the Soka University of America Board of Trustees], who did her doctorate on *The Plum in the Golden Vase,* to explain the attraction of Chinese literature. She replied that Chinese literature is characterized by a creative energy replete with a profound love of humanity, an assessment with which I agree. I believe this was one reason why Toda employed Chinese literature to train and foster young people.

LAU: Among the English-language books I read were those by William Shakespeare, George Bernard Shaw, the Brontë sisters, etc. I particularly liked *The Adventures of Tom Sawyer* by Mark

Twain, *David Copperfield* by Charles Dickens, and *The Three Mus-keteers* by Alexandre Dumas. I also read the Japanese classic *The Tale of Genji.*

My favorite characters in all my youthful readings are Sun Wukong of *Travels to the West*, Zhuge Liang of *The Romance of the Three Kingdoms*, Tom Sawyer, and d'Artagnan of *The Three Mus-keteers*. Sun Wukong is unconventional, a rebel, and yet I admire his commitment, loyalty, persistence, and resourcefulness. The same goes for Tom Sawyer. Zhuge Liang is a traditional Chinese scholar—I admire his total dedication, loyalty, and selflessness, and of course his grand vision, brilliant strategies, and inge-nious tactics. D'Artagnan is similar, though much less of a grand strategist.

I would say that Zhuge Liang is, in many ways, my role model. I strive to serve the people of my country in the same way that he did.

Ikeda: Thank you for your succinct, perceptive, and insightful description of the essential traits of these literary characters.

We can enrich our lives without limit by exploring our inner depths, developing ourselves from within, and elevating the way we lead our lives. This is what is described in Buddhism as the expansive potential of one's state of life.

One of the real pleasures of reading good books is that, by tak-ing the heroes and other characters as our models, we can culti-vate and inform a new self within. We can also awaken to more exalted goals in life and discover new paths to pursue.

Jin Yong has called on young people to continue reading over a lifetime. Reading certainly strengthens, deepens, and brightens our lives. Toda also urged young people to read good books and familiarize themselves with outstanding literature. This is why I also constantly stress the importance of reading when speaking with young people, including the students of Soka University, Soka Women's College, and the Soka schools.[2]

THE ROMANCE OF THE THREE KINGDOMS

LAU: In this regard, I would like to share with you a Chinese poem that I wrote in 2007:

隨緣不隨俗
無求亦有求
功名若塵土
只為天下憂

It can be approximately translated into English as follows:

I follow no conventions, but go wherever fate takes me;
I want nothing, and yet I have a purpose;
Fame and success are like earth and dust to me—
I only want to look out for my country.

President Ikeda, I know you are a great poet. I would greatly appreciate your comments and suggestions on both the Chinese and English versions.

IKEDA: First of all, I'm inspired by your desire expressed earlier to strive to serve the people of your country. And regarding your wonderful poem, it would be presumptuous of me to provide any advice. I am moved by this verse, which crystallizes your passion and commitment, as it is drawn from Zhuge Liang, on whom you model your life. He cared deeply for his country and continued to exercise leadership even when fatally ill.

I still remember Toda's thoughts on Zhuge Liang, one of the

main characters in the Chinese epic *The Romance of the Three Kingdoms*. As I wrote in my novel *The Human Revolution*, we, representatives of his young disciples, sang *"Hoshiotsu shufu gojogen"* (A Star Falls in the Autumn Wind on Wuchang Plain) for Toda one day during the New Year's holidays. This song was composed by the renowned Japanese poet Bansui Doi to convey the desperate thoughts of the dying Zhuge Liang, who had led his army in the Battle of Wuchang Plain.

> The autumn wind, with deepening sorrow, blows from
>   Mount Ch'i.
> Gloomy clouds gather over the battleground
> of Wuchang Plain.
>
> . . . .
>
> The Regent is deathly ill.
>
> . . . .
>
> Who could dispute the success or failure—
> Of the loyal man who gave his life?
>
> . . . .
>
> Are they illuminating the hero's
> Solitary heart loyal yet distressed?
> Moved by his bravery
> Even a demon wails in the autumn wind.
>
> . . . .
>
> Thousand years passed till now,
> Yet remains high the renown of [Zhuge] Liang.[3]

When we had finished, Toda asked us to sing it again and again, finally telling us: "Do you understand the true spirit of this poem? It is not as simple as you may think. Even now I can clearly hear the voice of [Zhuge Liang] as he howls at heaven and wails at the earth.

Toda continued, saying: "The poem we just heard describes the spiritual anguish of [Zhuge Liang] as he neared death . . . . What strikes me most are the sense of responsibility as well as the inner struggle of a person who is aware of his own mission and who stands alone to carry out that mission."

In fact, my mentor explained, Zhuge Liang's very life hung by a thread. The army that he led was mired in a war that was all but lost.

"What can a person think and how would he feel if he finds himself in such a critical dilemma?" Toda asked us. "Certainly, his feelings would not be at all sentimental, much less resigned . . . . [Zhuge Liang's] tenacity of purpose on his deathbed is still alive in history."[4]

Through the example of Zhuge Liang's distress, Toda was expressing his own deepest feelings, standing up alone for the welfare of all people amid the ruins of a Japan devastated by war.

One time, while discussing *The Romance of the Three Kingdoms* from various perspectives, he identified Zhuge Liang and Liu Bei[5] as idealists and commented on the tragedy that they were defeated in the novel by realists such as Cao Cao.[6] There is always a conflict between idealists and realists. Ideals that fail to see reality are nothing but delusions. Realism without ideals allows the ugliest aspects of human society to triumph and cannot motivate us to create a better world.

This is why *The Romance of the Three Kingdoms* shows us the importance of both idealism and realism, and moving step by step closer to the ideal within the real world.

From your own experience, Professor Lau, given such lessons imparted by fine literature, at what age should children be introduced to good books?

THE FIRST SEVEN YEARS

LAU: I believe the best way to teach young people cultural heritage and values is to start from the time when they are very young, before they even begin kindergarten. Cultural heritage can be transmitted to our youth through stories, games, and exemplary behavior, long before they have learned to read and write. I remember being taught to recite the *Three Character Sutra* and *The Three Hundred Tang Poems* long before I had any idea what they meant. But in retrospect, it was a gift—I am most grateful that I learned these classics.

Literacy is of course important, but the transmission of culture and values does not depend solely on literacy. Having said this, I also know that I benefitted greatly from my own voluminous readings in my youth—I learned about situations that extended far beyond my personal experiences.

IKEDA: The British historian Arnold J. Toynbee, with whom I had the privilege of engaging in dialogue, shared your opinion that children should be introduced to good books from an early age. He said he felt as if the first seven years of his life were as long as all his remaining years combined. Children should learn what is important to them in these first seven years, he said.

He also reflected:

> My mother awakened in me a life-long interest in History by communicating to me her own interest in it at a very early stage of my life. At the youngest age to which my memory can travel back, I was already possessed, thanks to what my mother had by then already done for me, by a love for History which has never left me.[7]

Professor Toynbee's mother would recount the events of English history to him as his bedtime stories.[8] The first seven years of existence may indeed be the most formative period in a child's life.

In discussions with many educators, I have affirmed the importance of reading fairy tales and other stories to young children and encouraging them to read for themselves. This belief in the value of education during such a crucial period in a child's life was instrumental in my founding kindergartens not only in Japan and Hong Kong but also in Singapore, Malaysia, Brazil, and South Korea.

Returning to an earlier subject, it must have been quite trying and worrisome for your mother to be apart from you and your older brother after the rest of your family moved to Taiwan.

THE EXTRA MILE

LAU: Before I return to talking about my mother, let me say that I agree with Professor Toynbee 100 percent. Knowing history, especially one's own national history, is critical to having a sense of self and a sense of belonging to a culture and a nation.

Returning to my mother, her health was never very robust. Sadly, she had a heart attack in her sleep and passed away on Chinese New Year's Day in Taipei in 1960, when I was fifteen. The entire family was in Taipei then for the celebration of the Chinese New Year. We were all in shock. After my mother's funeral service, my father gathered all of us together and told us that he did not have much wealth, not many financial or material assets, but that he had many friends, and that these friends were his wealth, his assets.

IKEDA: Her sudden death must have grieved you all terribly. But your father told you and your brothers that he had many good friends. Friendship is life's greatest treasure—with this message, he not only sought to encourage and inspire you, he also moved forward intrepidly himself.

I am sure that now, so many years later, your mother would be delighted at the achievements of you and your siblings. Your brilliant contributions to society and the welfare of others stand as a testament to your parents' triumphant lives.

LAU: Thank you. Speaking of which, on another occasion, my father told me that with friends one should always go the extra mile, that it is not enough to do only what is proper and legally required, that one should try to do even more to help one's friends. "Go the extra mile for your friends" is advice that I have always taken to heart. My father has always been gracious and generous to his friends—he picks up the tab whenever he eats out at restaurants with friends, and he gives things away freely to any friend who likes anything that he has.

My father is always courteous and friendly to everyone. Even though he always wears a bow tie, he is easy-going and has no airs. Deep down, he is a person of strongly held principles, over which he never compromises. He is what one would describe as "round on the outside and square on the inside." It is also a trait I try to emulate.

My father never remarried after the death of my mother more than half a century ago. He dedicated himself selflessly to raising my four brothers and me. He made sure that all of us would have at least a university education—despite the significant costs. Eddy, John, Patrick, and I all had the opportunity to pursue advanced studies in the United States; Taiching is the only brother who never studied abroad. Even then, he had many opportunities to travel to foreign countries. My brothers and I owe our father a great debt that can never be fully repaid.

IKEDA: I can see that your father held firmly to the belief that education is the best gift one can impart to one's children—and, in reply, you and your siblings have wholeheartedly embraced your father's hopes and wishes by dedicating yourselves to the task of scholarship.

No one is exempt from the trials that fate imposes on our lives. Yet, to carry on without bowing to defeat, no matter what one may encounter—this is most important. Your father prevailed over inexpressible grief to selflessly serve not only his family but others. The example he set with his life has been the foremost support in your lives and represents the finest education he could provide.

As a university founder myself, I have encountered numerous parents who have managed to put their children through college out of their honorable desire to provide their offspring with a quality education, regardless of the difficulties they would shoulder. This is why I have shared the following points with the students of our Soka schools, Soka Women's College, and Soka University whenever possible: that one truly educated understands the depths of concern one's parents have for their children; that one who has undergone a human-centric education should strive to remain on the best of terms with siblings to reassure one's parents; and that dedicating oneself to learning is synonymous with filial piety and fulfilling one's debt of gratitude.

The narrative of your life will undoubtedly serve as an immense source of courage and inspiration, not only for students enduring manifold difficulties in their youth but for their parents.

CONVERSATION FIVE

The Path of Friendship

IKEDA: I understand Yu Youren was a major benefactor of education, serving as one of the founders of Fudan University in Shanghai. I have visited the school three times, and they were all memorable occasions for me.[1]

A stirring narrative of the mentor-disciple relationship between Yu Youren and his teacher Ma Xiangbo, one of China's foremost educators, is part of the history of Fudan University's founding. Would you be so kind as to recount the story of these two illustrious individuals?

LAU: As you mentioned earlier (see Conversation One), I have presented you with a book reproducing Grandfather Yu's calligraphy, *Master of Cursive Calligraphy: Yu Youren 1879–1964*. The original works are at Fudan University.

IKEDA: Thank you for this precious gift. The Chinese have long regarded calligraphy as a visual representation of the individual's spirit and believed that if one's character is sound, one's brushwork will be impeccable. Calligraphy really does express an individual's character.

Yu Youren was praised as possessing the character of a sage and being an expert in the cursive style of calligraphy. I was inspired upon viewing his work reproduced in the book you presented me.

When, as a young man, Yu was persecuted by the authorities for speaking out for his beliefs, his teacher Ma Xiangbo staunchly stood up for him and enabled Yu to study at Zhendan Xueyuan (Aurora University), which Ma founded and administered.

Lau: In fact, Grandfather Yu was put on a "wanted list" by the Qing government. He was to be executed forthwith if the authorities caught him. Ma Xiangbo provided Grandfather Yu refuge, sheltering him as a student at Zhendan Xueyuan.

Ikeda: Eventually, foreign authorities unjustly interfered with the academy, which put Ma in a dilemma, forcing him to step down as its president. Yu Youren vowed to repay his profound debt of gratitude to Ma Xiangbo by reopening the academy, something his mentor longed to see, and reinstating him in his former post. After overcoming numerous obstacles, Yu joined his comrade in 1905 to found a new school and welcomed his teacher as its president. He proposed that the new school be called Fudan Public School, the name Fudan connoting China's revival and paying tribute to Zhendan Xueyuan"[2] This, as I understand, is the story behind the university's establishment. Is it correct?

Lau: Yes, that's completely correct.

Ikeda: Ma Xiangbo died during the Second Sino-Japanese War. Later, Yu Youren inscribed the title calligraphy for Ma Xiangbo's published research and purchased numerous copies to distribute to various libraries, thus promoting his teacher's reputation. I was moved to learn of their shared triumph, which characterized Yu Youren's life, a triumph that left a lasting impression on me.

As a youth, I served my mentor, and I have ever since dedicated my life to communicating to the entire world the greatness of his accomplishments and way of life. This is why I can empathize with Yu's sentiments on a personal level. Yu's achievements stand as a vital lesson for us all, particularly for youth.

LAU: Grandfather Yu was very much older than me; if he were alive today, he'd be more than 130 years old.

I have the following memory of him: One day, he was asked to write a memoir. He declared that he had no wish to do so, saying if he wrote the truth, he was bound to hurt someone's feelings; and if he didn't write the truth, there was no point in writing a memoir. He never did write anything resembling a memoir or autobiography—a fact that reflects his character.

Grandfather Yu liked very simple foods, such as noodles, and wore only clothes and shoes made of cloth. He practiced calligraphy every day. He never had any money and lived quite frugally, eschewing any luxury. In his home in Taipei, there was no flush toilet.

Grandfather Yu had no airs and treated everyone equally, irrespective of his or her rank or station in life. He was completely accessible to the common citizen. He frequently received invitations to luncheons and dinners, and his practice was to always accept the first invitation and not to discriminate on the basis of position or wealth of the person issuing the invitation.

YU YOUREN'S COMPASSION

IKEDA: In the words of Yu Youren, "Money is like dung." Gishin Nishide, a scholar of Yu's calligraphy, took that as the title for his insightful biography on Yu, which was published to commemorate the centennial of the Chinese Revolution of 1911.

Nishide wrote that, in his final years, Yu had a metal box he wanted opened after his death. This was done, and inside were three volumes of a diary from his last years, letters, and some scribbled notes, one of which was an accounting of loans he made to help needy friends and students.

He had cared nothing about money and led a frugal life, using his earnings to help those facing financial distress. Though Yu's calligraphic works sold for handsome sums even while he was alive, he often readily gave them away to those who expressed a desire for them, saying that the act of creating the calligraphy itself brought him indescribable joy.[3]

Nishide's description of Yu reveals his pure, selfless character. Did you see him often when you were in Taiwan?

LAU: I believe one of the notes recorded a loan he had taken out to enable a son of his (and an uncle of mine) to pursue his graduate studies in the United States.

My parents and Grandfather Yu lived in the same house in Taipei. I saw him almost every summer, when I went to Taipei for vacation. But I was too young then to have a meaningful conversation with him. I do wish that I had been more interested in Chinese calligraphy then; I would have asked him to write many more pieces for me. And had I known more about Chinese history, I would have asked him more questions.

In 2005, my cousins, all the grandchildren of Grandfather Yu, and I started the Yu Youren Calligraphic Gallery at Fudan University by lending to it our personal collections of Grandfather Yu's calligraphic pieces.

Grandfather Yu participated in the Chinese Revolution of 1911. He served in the interim government of the Republic of China organized by Dr. Sun Yat-sen as the vice minister of communications during the first year of the Republic. He subsequently served as the president of the Control Yuan for more than thirty years. However, many years from now, I believe Grandfather Yu will be remembered not as a revolutionary and not as a government official, but as a calligrapher who promoted and standardized cursive Chinese calligraphy, the first time in many centuries.

IKEDA: On another subject, Nishide's scholarly biography also records an episode from the friendship between Yu Youren and Chinese Premier Zhou Enlai. Yu spent his last years in Taiwan, but his wife remained in mainland China. And it pained him deeply that he could not celebrate her eightieth birthday with her. Learning of this, Premier Zhou arranged for a festive celebration for Yu's wife. When Yu conveyed his gratitude, the premier is said to have replied: "As long as you are happy, that alone is worthwhile. It also brings us peace of mind." I believe the friendship forged between these two men endured because it transcended both ideology and standing.

Yu was a sturdy man, but as he aged, his legs grew frail. In spite of that, when people came to visit him on his birthdays, even if they were fairly young, he always stood up to greet them and shake their hands. Though people urged him to remain seated in such cases, he refused, saying it wasn't polite. There are countless stories of this nature regarding Yu Youren.

I once had the opportunity to see a passage from the *Mozi*, the principal work left by the Chinese philosopher Mozi, in Yu's calligraphy. It read, "We must feed the hungry, clothe the cold, give the weary rest, and the disturbed peace."[4] It was an unconstrained, sublime, and highly animated work of calligraphy, but the strongest impression it gave me was of compassion for the people.

LAU: What I respect most about Grandfather Yu is that he always put the interests of the common people first. His consistent goal was to improve people's livelihoods and his preferred long-term instrument was education at all levels.

In his youth, he was responsible for running soup (actually congee) kitchens to feed the people affected by famines in the region around Xian. When he was the administrator of Shaanxi Province in the early twentieth century, he authorized the construction of waterworks for irrigation and flood control, established agricultural research and extension stations to improve local crop yields, created jobs, reduced taxes, and established primary and secondary educational institutions and at least one tertiary educational institution in the province.

He also helped establish many universities in China, including Fudan University, Northwest Agriculture and Forestry University, and the University of Shanghai. Anticorruption was one of the principal objectives of the Control Yuan, which he led for more than thirty years. Eliminating or even just reducing corruption of government officials would go a long way toward improving the livelihood of the common people.

FAITH AND PRACTICE

LAU: Let me ask you a few questions for a change. I understand that the Soka Gakkai, not only in Japan but also Hong Kong, was founded on Buddhist principles, such as those in the Lotus Sutra. (My father is a Buddhist, as was my late mother.) However, it appears, at least to an outsider like myself, that the Soka Gakkai seems to be free of the traditional Buddhist practices—there do not seem to be temples, statues of Buddhas, monks or nuns, or even Buddhist priests, nor prohibitions against the consumption of meat. It is unlike any traditional, organized Buddhism or, for that matter, any other organized religion anywhere.

Can you tell me how members of the Soka Gakkai learn the Buddhist principles and how they practice their religion?

IKEDA: When I heard that your parents were devout Buddhists, I immediately felt a rapport with them. And, as a fellow Buddhist, I felt moved to offer a prayer for the peaceful repose of your late mother.

As you know, our organization, the Soka Gakkai International, has grown to encompass a vast network of members in 192 countries and territories, including Hong Kong. My fellow SGI members and I practice the teachings of Nichiren Buddhism, which follow the core principles of the Lotus Sutra. In doing so, we engage in initiatives to further peace, advance education, and promote cultural awareness and appreciation.

In my view, what is important in practicing our faith is that we never lose sight of Buddhism's fundamental spirit. By this, I mean that we must be ever mindful of the essential reason Shakyamuni Buddha appeared in this world and why he devoted his entire life to expounding his teachings. The Buddha illuminates this point in the "Expedient Means" chapter of the Lotus Sutra: "At the start I took a vow, / hoping to make all persons / equal to me, without any distinction between us."[5]

In essence, he taught that a Buddha's fundamental aim is to elevate the life-state of ordinary people to that of Buddhahood. As the basis for this, he revealed that every person is endowed with the Buddha nature and that, for this reason, all people are equal to one another and can achieve a life-state of Buddhahood, or enlightenment.

The Great Teacher Tiantai, or Zhiyi, a Chinese sage in the sixth century, discerned that the basis of all Buddhist thought lies in this teaching of universal enlightenment, and he extolled the Lotus Sutra, which expounded this principle, as Buddhism's supreme scripture.

Then, in the thirteenth century, Nichiren discovered that the Law enabling all people to attain Buddhahood, the Law of universal enlightenment, is Nam-myoho-renge-kyo,[6] the phrase embodying the Lotus Sutra's essence. In other words, Nichiren identified the fundamental Law of life and the universe as Nam-myoho-renge-kyo and the chanting of Nam-myoho-renge-kyo as the practice for attaining Buddhahood. This practice is accessible to everyone, so that we can manifest the Buddha nature inherent in our lives.

And this is why the daily practice of SGI members centers around chanting Nam-myoho-renge-kyo. We also recite, every morning and evening, essential portions of the "Expedient Means" and "Life Span" chapters of the Lotus Sutra that hold the sutra's most important principles.

LAU: Is that how SGI members put their faith into practice, then?

IKEDA: Yes. This may seem somewhat esoteric, but simply put, when we recite the "Expedient Means" and "Life Span" chapters of the sutra and chant Nam-myoho-renge-kyo, we face a mandala of ideograms known as the Gohonzon,[7] which Nichiren inscribed as our object of devotion. As to this object of devotion, Nichiren said, "I, Nichiren, have inscribed my life in sumi [black Chinese] ink, so believe in the Gohonzon with your whole heart."[8] The Gohonzon thus embodies his enlightened life of Buddhahood.

The Gohonzon's ideograms depict the Ceremony in the Air,[9] a metaphoric assembly of bodhisattvas[10] before the treasure tower described in the "Treasure Tower" chapter of the Lotus Sutra. The Ceremony in the Air symbolizes the Law of universal enlightenment, or Nam-myoho-renge-kyo, the essence of the Lotus Sutra. Based on this Law, every person can draw forth the compassion and wisdom of Buddhahood inherent in him- or herself. By believing in the Gohonzon and chanting Nam-myoho-renge-kyo, all people can reveal and develop the treasure tower—that is, the Buddha nature—in their own life.

Nichiren explained to one of his lay followers, Abutsu-bo:

> In the Latter Day of the Law, no treasure tower exists other
> than the figures of the men and women who embrace the

Lotus Sutra. It follows, therefore, that whether eminent or humble, high or low, those who chant Nam-myoho-renge-kyo are themselves the treasure tower, and, likewise, are themselves the Thus Come One Many Treasures.[11]

Faith in the Gohonzon is the basis of our Buddhist practice.

Another significant aspect of the Ceremony in the Air: This is the ceremony where the bodhisattvas pledge to share the Buddha's eternal vow for the enlightenment of all people and, as his disciples, to fulfill this earnest desire in the world. Thus, praying to the Gohonzon is synonymous with vowing to help realize the happiness of humankind and world peace.

For a Buddhist practitioner, attaining Buddhahood merely for oneself is not the ultimate objective. On a much deeper level, it is to embrace the Buddha's great desire as one's own and engage in the grand, altruistic undertaking to eliminate suffering as a lifelong mission.

The Lotus Sutra depicts the developmental struggles of Shakyamuni's disciples. It is a dramatic narrative in which they evolve from individuals who seek enlightenment for themselves to individuals who, with deep resolve, strive to enable others to achieve enlightenment. One who embraces this altruistic practice, or bodhisattva way, of Mahayana Buddhism seeks the happiness of both oneself and others, and therefore finds it impossible to turn away from suffering people. This sense of altruistic compassion is the heart and soul of Nichiren Buddhism. To live as a bodhisattva constitutes our Buddhist practice.

Nichiren Buddhism

Lau: How do SGI members study such Buddhist principles in daily life?

IKEDA: We study them through Nichiren's writings, such as his Buddhist treatises, some of which are composed as dialogues, and the letters he wrote to his disciples and followers. We diligently study his writings to deepen our understanding of and insight into Buddhist teachings; they provide the guiding foundations of our practice. This is the element of study in our faith. Nichiren wrote: "Without practice and study, there can be no Buddhism. . . . Both practice and study arise from faith."[12] The three elements of faith, practice, and study are considered the fundamentals for the practice of Buddhism as taught by Nichiren.

Since Makiguchi's day, the foundation of the Soka Gakkai's activities has been the discussion meeting. At these meetings, participants study the Buddhist teachings, share their faith experiences, and draw inspiration from one another as they strengthen their relationships through dialogue.

The American philosopher Lou Marinoff has recognized the value of SGI discussion meetings, emphasizing the importance of dialogue among members. In fact, he explained, philosophers should engage in their discipline from precisely the same perspective as the SGI discussion meeting—through the sharing of experience one gains a richer and more expansive view of humankind. He said that listening to what others have to say enables one to nurture a deeper understanding of oneself. His belief is that Buddhism presents a viable means with which one can discover the power inherent in the self.[13]

Discussion meetings are held virtually every month in the SGI around the world. And regardless of where they are held, you will find inspiring scenes in which people of every age, race, ethnicity, and language engage one another in conversation and share a sense of camaraderie.

Shakyamuni Buddha taught the importance of cultivating "good friends," stating that this "constitutes all of the Buddha Way."[14]

Our organization brings together such friends, bonded through their Buddhist faith. They advance their own happiness and that of others while working over the years to promote a united community for peace throughout the world.

Nichiren wrote, "The Buddha surely considers anyone in this world who embraces the Lotus Sutra, whether lay man or woman, monk or nun, to be the lord of all living beings."[15] He also underscored the importance of gender equality: "There should be no discrimination among those who propagate . . . the Law, be they men or women."[16] By these statements, he meant that every person who embraces his teachings shares equally in a sacred mission. In Nichiren Buddhism, there is no inherent distinction between persons based on race, ethnicity, social status, gender, or between clergy and laity.

Toynbee noted the following:

> In the heritage of each of the higher religions we are aware of the presence of two kinds of ingredients. There are essential counsels and truths, and there are nonessential practices and propositions.[17]

While Toynbee used "higher religions," I believe he also meant "world religions." He went on to say that these "essential counsels and truths" are "valid at all times and places." In other words, he was referring to an enduring universal philosophy.

As members of a Buddhist lay organization, we have remained firmly committed to the spirit of the Law of universal enlightenment, which lies at the heart of the "essential counsels and truths" of the Lotus Sutra. This is why our Buddhist movement has flourished in modern society and expanded worldwide, giving people hope and courage.

CHINA-JAPAN RELATIONS

LAU: The next question I would like to ask relates to China-Japan relations. To preface this question, I believe the Chinese and Japanese economies are highly complementary. Each typically produces and exports goods that are not produced in or imported from the other. I believe a China-Japan free trade agreement can be of great benefit to both countries, precisely because the economies of both countries are so different. In contrast, a Japan-South Korea free trade area will result in far fewer benefits for both sides because the industries in both economies are quite similar and competitive—automobiles, steel, cell phones, etc.

Do you think a China-Japan FTA will eventually be possible?

IKEDA: Given the gravity of the issue, I should be asking you, the expert, for your opinion! Although 2013 marked the thirty-fifth anniversary of the signing of the Japan-China Treaty of Peace and Friendship, our bilateral relationship has regrettably chilled to such a degree that it has been described as the worst it has been since the end of World War II. In my SGI peace proposal[18] published on January 26, 2013, I called for the two countries to reaffirm the two central pledges stated in the treaty—to refrain from the use or threat of force, and to not seek regional hegemony—and upon doing so, hold high-level discussions at the earliest possible opportunity.

No one can deny that China's presence is monumental, both for the future of the Japanese economy and for the development of the global economy. I also believe that relations with China are vital to Japan's interests, and that it is equally vital that this bilateral relationship be friendly and fortified, not only in the economic sphere but in every realm.

In 1968, when Japan's trade with China was practically nonexistent and diplomatic relations had still not been normalized, I called for the normalization of bilateral ties before a large gathering of college students in the Soka Gakkai, pointing out that the expansion of Sino-Japanese trade would lead directly to both nations' prosperity (see Appendix 1). While bilateral ties are strained today, I am struck by how the situation has changed since then. Japan's net imports and exports climbed to some $1.3 trillion in 2013, and by far, the largest share of that was trade with China. Moreover, this figure exceeds the amount of trade with the United States, Japan's second major trading partner, by some 50 percent. From this fact alone, it is clear that trade with China is a central pillar supporting the Japanese economy.

Since the Cold War's end, amid the rapidly increasing pace of globalization, we have seen a steady escalation in trade liberalization in East Asia as well as among the member-states of the Association of Southeast Asian Nations. Meanwhile, South Korea has sought and concluded FTAs with other countries. The number of FTAs concluded by Japan as well as by China also increased year by year, a trend that is expected to accelerate.

No system is from the start without flaws, however, so it is vital that countries try to strengthen their relationships where possible and negotiate as equals, with consideration and empathy for the position and struggles of the other side. First and foremost, the greatest care must be taken to make sure that the new trade regime will not inflict economic hardship on people or industries. This is the primary responsibility that political leaders must bear.

When reviewing the prospects for a Japan-China FTA, I believe it is important to scrutinize examples of similar arrangements concluded by other countries around the world. And in light of the issues identified through this examination, to thoroughly explore ways to establish the foundation for a trading system that creates mutual benefit and win-win cooperation.

LAU: I believe a China-Japan free trade area is one possibility that is win-win, given the high degree of economic complementarity between the two economies. Another possibility is exchange-rate coordination between China and Japan in a way similar to what has been proposed by Professor Robert Mundell, Nobel laureate in economic sciences, for the US dollar and the euro.

Stability of the East Asian economies can be greatly enhanced if there is some real exchange-rate coordination among them. In particular, if the yuan and the yen can maintain a relative real parity, it is likely that the currencies of other East Asian economies will follow suit, and this relative exchange-rate stability can greatly facilitate the growth of international trade and foreign direct investment in East Asia. And it will also over time reduce the dependence of East Asian economies on the use of the US dollar as a medium of international exchange.

Again, do you think such developments are possible?

THE YEN-YUAN EXCHANGE

IKEDA: Actually, this is an issue that I raised more than forty years ago in an article on ways to facilitate normalized relations between Japan and China for a monthly magazine.[19] I called for the reevaluation of the international settlement regime based on the then-unstable British pound sterling. In its place, I proposed instituting a system advocated by China, which would rely on the yen and yuan as settlement currencies. I also emphasized that decisions must be based on the principle of mutual prosperity and the establishment of reciprocal relationships.[20]

In recent years, a succession of global economic crises has struck, defying conventional wisdom. These concurrent shocks— led by the collapse of Lehman Brothers and loss of confidence in the dollar and concern over the strength of the euro, which had been a candidate to become the world's secondary reserve currency—have spilled over into the global economy, leaving no country unaffected.

In the early 1970s, I discussed with Toynbee the dollar-based reserve currency system. At the time, America was struggling under the weight of massive outlays spent on the Vietnam War, and its position in the global economy was suffering markedly. Naturally, the dollar's unstable value had substantially undermined the global economic order. Toynbee expressed his doubts about a currency system that is vulnerable to fluctuation in economic conditions of a single country. He thought that a reliable, secure world currency must be "based on something that, unlike gold, has an intrinsic, practical value that is both stable and high."[21]

Nearly half a century later, we have yet to resolve the concerns we had then, and I cannot help being reminded of how convoluted these issues are. While there remains little choice but to maintain the international monetary system as it is for the time being, there is a paramount need to devise effective strategies for resolving the issues we face.

LAU: Mr. Ikeda, you were way ahead of your time to have proposed the use of the yen and yuan as settlement currencies for international transactions forty years ago. It shows great insight on your part. And I believe we have finally arrived at the time to implement your original idea.

For example, China and Japan can agree to maintain the yen-yuan exchange rate within a range of, say, 15 to 18 yen per yuan. When the exchange rate falls below that rate range, the Bank of Japan will intervene by selling yen and buying yuan to keep it at 15 yen per yuan and prevent the yen from appreciating further with respect to the yuan. The Bank of Japan will have the incentive to do so because this will help maintain the competitiveness of Japanese exports in the Chinese market. When the exchange rate rises above 18 yen per yuan, the People's Bank of China will intervene by selling yuan and buying yen to keep the yuan from appreciating too much and hence reducing the competitiveness of Chinese exports in the Japanese market. Thus, excess volatility in the yen-yuan exchange rate can be avoided, which will facilitate the growth of trade and direct investment flows between the two countries.

Over time, if this scheme proves successful, the range of fluctuation of the relative exchange rate can be narrowed, further facilitating the growth of trade and direct investment flows between China and Japan. It is also possible to have this type of exchange rate coordination in real terms—instead of maintaining the relative nominal exchange rate within an agreed range, the relative real exchange rate, taking into account the changes in the relative rates of inflation of the two countries, is maintained within an agreed range.

IKEDA: As you point out, in order to facilitate a sustainable relationship for bilateral trade, the time has come to devise measures to support a stable exchange rate between the yen and yuan. Such measures will not only contribute to the economic development of both countries but will certainly have a positive influence in stabilizing the regional economy of Asia.

In June 2011, a system for direct yen-yuan settlement of payments, though the number of transactions was limited, was launched. It eliminates the cost of currency exchange transactions intermediated in dollars while remaining basically unhindered by uncertainties over the dollar's strength or weakness. The volume of transactions can be expected to rise over time. I hope that this kind of direct settlement system can become a test bed to evaluate the concept's validity.

JAPAN'S FUTURE ECONOMY

IKEDA: It's widely believed that Japan—saddled as it is by such manifold and serious issues as securing an economic recovery and righting its public finances—has entered a critical juncture in its development. What is your assessment of the Japanese economy today? And what do you propose Japan do to improve its lot?

LAU: The Japanese economy needs more aggregate demand. Given the size of the Japanese economy and the state of the world economy, a significant increase in Japanese aggregate demand can only come from a significant increase in domestic demand. How can Japan create a significant increase in domestic demand that will drive the Japanese economy forward?

One idea that I have suggested calls for the Japanese government to promote the re-housing of Japanese households in urban centers. Currently, housing for the typical Japanese household has two problems: First, there is too little space; and second, it is located too far away from the urban centers.

Given the Japanese per capita GDP, Japanese people ought to live in much more space per person than they do now. Moreover, the typical Japanese worker spends at least two hours, often more, commuting each day between home and the workplace. The quality of life of the typical Japanese worker can be greatly improved if the distance between home and the workplace can be significantly reduced. There will be more time for the family to enjoy life together.

Thus, if the old urban centers are re-built to provide housing—with, say, twice as much space per household as is currently the case—and the suburban households all move back into the urban centers, there will be a huge construction boom that can last a couple decades, with derivative demands for appliances and furniture. The re-urbanization itself will also create new demands and new supplies of services. GDP and employment will rise, and the overall quality of life will be significantly enhanced. Of course, the suburbs will lose population, but the lower population density may enable larger and more efficient farms, taking advantage of the benefits of mechanization and economies of scale.

IKEDA: You raise a good point about how urban redevelopment can drive domestic consumption and economic growth in Japan.

In your view, which industries does Japan excel in? And how do you think they can achieve greater growth in the future?

LAU: The Japanese people are perfectionists. Japanese professionalism and quality are major selling points. In addition to manufacturing, Japan has a long tradition of producing outstanding artisanal products of the highest quality—for example, ceramics, sake, and *wagyu* beef. It is the leading creator and originator of anime. These products should be more widely introduced to the world.

Japan can also provide the best services to the world; for example, auditing services and quality assurance. Your country is well known for its quality control. W. Edwards Deming's emphasis on quality assurance and control had a huge impact on the Japanese manufacturing industry. This is perhaps another field in which China-Japan cooperation is possible.

Japan must promote innovation. Japan has brought to the world such new consumer products as the Walkman, Watchman, PlayStation, the compact disc, the digital camera, and the videotape machine. It must continue to innovate.

However, in general, East Asians, including the Chinese, Japanese, and Koreans, have too much respect for authority and for the establishment to question conventional wisdom and challenge the status quo. It is precisely through questioning accepted wisdom that innovative breakthroughs are made. Albert Einstein would not have been able to discover the theory of relativity if he had not questioned Isaac Newton's Laws of Motion. I believe this respect for authority and respect for the elder are ingrained in the East Asian culture and will take a long time to change.

Japan should encourage young Japanese students to go abroad for their college education and welcome their return. This way, they may acquire and develop new and different ideas and will be much more likely to become breakthrough innovators.

Japan can also do more to promote entrepreneurship. In 2013, the number of new patents granted by the United States to Japanese nationals was 51,919, second only to that of the United States, with its home advantage, of 133,593. However, Japan's competitive edge in patents granted does not seem to translate into commercially successful innovation as in the United States and other economies. I believe there is great economic potential if Japan were to adopt policies that more actively encouraged entrepreneurship and helped create an environment friendlier and more hospitable to start-ups and new enterprises.

Prospects for East Asia

LAU: With the establishment of the European Union in 1993, Europe has shown us how economic cooperation can eventually lead to political accommodation and cooperation. France and Germany, which fought three major wars against one another within eighty years, are now permanent allies. Do you think a similar development is possible within East Asia?

IKEDA: In 1967 and 1970, I had the privilege of conducting a dialogue with Count Coudenhove-Kalergi, the Austrian thinker and pioneering proponent of European unification. He stated at the time that Europe, even though composed of separate countries, was actually one entity. As such, it was his hope that Europe would, as a united community, maintain peaceful, friendly ties with the United States and the former Soviet Union.[1]

More than twenty years after we discussed the concept of a "united Europe," the European Communities—which was established (in 1967) on the basis of economic cooperation—would develop, evolve, and then eventually depart anew as the European Union. That a continent once rent by two world wars continues to integrate into a single entity represents a social experiment with historic ramifications for all humanity.

The EU was established with the aim of achieving political unity through economic integration, and its establishment has proven successful in terms of peace and stability in the region. On the other hand, as can be seen in the Eurozone crisis,[2] the EU is now facing new issues unique to regional integration and will have to make some difficult choices in order to navigate through these challenges.

While the major countries in East Asia have yet to conclude free trade agreements among one another, economic relationships, following the trend of the times, continue to strengthen. However, the underlying premise of these relationships should rest on bringing about harmonious coexistence and mutual prosperity.

As we know, in ASEAN, the exchange and negotiations between the member countries compiled over many years have enhanced stability within the region. For East Asia to achieve its own regional integration, I believe it is essential that we learn from the successful elements extant in the ASEAN framework.

LAU: The East Asian economies (and India) have had the good fortune of emerging from the global financial crisis of 2008 relatively unscathed. They have shown that they are capable of being partially decoupled from the developed economies of the West—they can continue growing even as the United States and Western Europe are in serious economic recession.

East Asia, defined as the area west of the Pacific Ocean and east of Bangladesh, now has a GDP as large as the United States. East Asia trades more with itself than with the rest of the world, signifying that it can grow sustainably on its own, even if the North American and European economies remain in relative stagnation. East Asian economies should resist the temptation to emulate the "financial innovation" practiced in the developed economies of the West (which led them into the global financial crisis of 2008).

It is possible for East Asian economies to better coordinate their policies. For example, they can try to maintain real relative parities of their exchange rates with one another, so that no one country or region tries to take advantage of the others by adopting a "beggar thy neighbor" policy.

And when it becomes necessary to adjust the exchange rates vis-à-vis the United States or Europe, the East Asian currencies can move up and down together, keeping their relative real exchange rate parities, and hence relative competitiveness, unchanged. This way, no one East Asian economy experiences gains or losses as a result of the collective revaluation or devaluation of their currencies. Stable relative real exchange rates, moreover, encourage the growth of international trade and long-term cross-country investment—both direct and portfolio—among the countries concerned.

EAST ASIAN INTEGRATION

IKEDA: So you believe that there is a way to coordinate economic policy among East Asian nations more efficiently. And if that is successfully done, we can expect the region's economy to grow on an even more stable and comprehensive basis.

LAU: East Asian nations can also try to devise a new settlement and clearing mechanism for international (trade and capital) transactions among themselves. Another problem they can tackle collectively is to devise a mechanism for discouraging short-term international capital inflows but encouraging long-term international capital inflows. Short-term capital inflows (whether in the form of loans or portfolio investments), unlike trade or direct investment flows, or long-term loans, do not bring much benefit to the recipient economy—and these flows cannot and should not be used to finance long-term projects.

The 1997–98 East Asian financial crisis was brought about precisely by over-reliance on short-term capital inflows, which almost instantly became short-term capital outflows at the first sign of trouble. Short-term capital flows can also bring much harm by increasing the volatility of the exchange rate of the recipient economy. East Asian economies, with the possible exception of the Philippines, all have high savings rates and do not really need short-term capital inflows. One way to discourage short-term capital inflows is to require the capital to stay in an interest-free or negative-interest-rate bank account for a year before it can be deployed for any other purpose. A "Tobin tax"—a tax on spot capital account currency conversions—is another possibility.

IKEDA: The East Asian financial crisis also forced millions in the region into dire economic straits. As you point out, we need to learn the lessons imparted by the crisis and prepare for every conceivable contingency to avoid such a disaster from ever happening again. In doing so, the East Asian countries will need to adopt a long-term outlook as they partner in developing solutions.

LAU: Another possible step is the formation of an "East Asian Monetary Fund." During the 1997–98 East Asian currency crisis, Japan actually proposed the formation of such an organization with the objective of helping the East Asian economies better survive the attacks of the hedge funds. Unfortunately, the United States blocked the Japanese effort. The results were catastrophic for such economies as Indonesia, South Korea, and Thailand.

I believe there is still room for such an organization that will not only serve as an emergency lender to the East Asian economies but also as the coordinator of relative exchange rates among them, playing the same role as the International Monetary Fund before the 1970s. If the exchange rates of the East Asian currencies can maintain stable relative real parities, it will greatly facilitate cross-border trade and investment. It will also become much easier for East Asian economies as a whole to adjust their exchange rates against major currencies such as the dollar and the euro.

IKEDA: I see that you are recommending that East Asia press ahead in establishing such a framework of cooperation and procedures. Given the complexities of the situation today, measures to promote mutual trust and confidence are urgent in building an integrated community.

The crux of these efforts should first be to establish a framework for cooperation on common challenges such as environmental issues and disaster response policies. And second, to encourage and enhance interpersonal exchange programs, with young people as the primary focus.

The East Asian countries have succeeded in attracting foreign capital, and many have achieved a remarkable degree of economic growth as a result. At the same time, this very success has spawned serious levels of environmental pollution and has become a source of great concern. I hope that a process that includes exchange among environmental experts can be put in motion and prioritized for prompt action to resolve this worldwide issue. I believe that Japan must take the initiative as a major contributor to this process, in terms of both technical and human resources.

Both the Great East Japan Earthquake and the Fukushima nuclear power plant accident in 2011[3] forced us to reexamine many major issues. Having experienced a natural disaster of such unimaginable magnitude, we became acutely aware of just how powerless we are as human beings. We were also forced to reaffirm that regional and international cooperation is indispensable when attempting to cope with such calamities.

As I mentioned earlier, soon after the disaster, many countries were generous with the support and cooperation they extended. This generosity and goodwill provided an inestimable measure of encouragement and strength to the stricken.

Disaster contingency initiatives that enable even faster cooperation among countries have become more imperative than ever before. In my view, such efforts are vital in enhancing mutual trust within a region.

Historically, the East Asian people have shared, to a great extent, a common cultural background and values. As we engage in the two key efforts I mentioned above and strive to engender mutual trust, we will begin to see the contours of an East Asian community come into clearer focus.

We must not fail in shaping East Asia into a region that forever renounces war. To achieve this objective, I am certain that such progressive moves as regional integration are well within the realm of possibility.

A NORTHEAST ASIAN NUCLEAR-FREE ZONE

LAU: I know you are an ardent believer in peace and harmony and a tireless advocate of universal nuclear disarmament. You are also an unwavering supporter of friendly relations between China and Japan. I share your objectives totally. However, how do you think we can bring them about?

IKEDA: Nuclear weapons and the specter of nuclear confrontation they pose are leading causes of increasing tension and instability in Northeast Asia. Given this situation, even if a country were prepared to reduce its nuclear arsenal, it would find it difficult to do so because of the extant nuclear threat in the region. The existence of this threat merely invites other countries to build up their militaries, thus emerging as new threats and fanning further tensions. We have seen this vicious cycle haunt Northeast Asia for decades.

I have long advocated, whenever possible, that the only way out of this dilemma is for the entire region to collectively sunder this self-destructive cycle, in which governments depend on nuclear weapons to ensure national security. In my 2009 proposal to abolish nuclear weapons,[4] I called for a policy initiative to make Northeast Asia a nuclear non-use region as a first step in this transformation.

One of the unique features of the region that is seriously complicating the denuclearization of Northeast Asia is this: All the countries engaged in the six-party talks on the North Korean nuclear program—the United States, Russia, China, Japan, South Korea, and North Korea—either possess nuclear weapons or are taking refuge under the nuclear umbrella extended by a nuclear-weapon state. Based on this, I suggested that all six parties to the talks offer mutual assurances neither to employ nuclear weapons against one another nor take actions that would heighten the threat posed by weapons of mass destruction. And that they should adopt this as an official "Nuclear Non-Use Region Declaration."

Regrettably, the current Treaty on the Non-Proliferation of Nuclear Weapons does not include any mechanisms to reduce the threat of nuclear weapons and enhance confidence on a mutual basis. All parties in regions living under the specter of nuclear attack would benefit if they were to strive toward adopting a regional nuclear non-use declaration or similar initiative to ease tension. Such an inclusive effort would create an environment in which every party came to believe that taking part in such a declaration would build more trust and enhance security. And that remaining a non-signatory would only deepen their sense of isolation.

I believe such a step represents a viable means with which to sever the ever-escalating cycle of threat and counter-threat. In considering this kind of cross-national effort, let me emphasize the importance, especially in a world of rapidly advancing globalization, of choosing inclusivity over exclusivity and multidimensionality over one-dimensionality.

In addition to working for the realization of a world without nuclear weapons, another twenty-first century issue to which Japan should devote its utmost is how best to contribute to the building of peace and stability in Asia. The pivotal element necessary to this task's success—as Zhou Enlai and I confirmed in our meeting, which I will cherish for as long as I live—rests with Japan and China forging bonds of friendship as robust as they are enduring.

It is time to put an end to an era of escalating confrontation, one in which countries have been locked in conflict over real and perceived threats, with fear begetting further fear and suspicion. As I mentioned earlier, it is now imperative to build relationships of trust among nations as we strive to work on common issues such as mitigating environmental problems and creating effective disaster contingency initiatives.

As to the issue of the environment, in my 2013 peace proposal, "Compassion, Wisdom and Courage: Building a Global Society of Peace and Creative Coexistence," I made the following a particular point of emphasis: Because bilateral relations are so strained at this time, it is imperative that the leaders of Japan and China craft conditions enabling them to come together and talk in person. I suggested the two countries should lay the foundations of a new partnership focused on peaceful coexistence and joint action for humanity's sake.

Among the specific initiatives I proposed was the launch of an organization, which could be named the East Asian Fund for Environmental Cooperation, under the coordinated leadership of both

Japan and China. Japan and China have worked together on the environment in the past, but I believe it is an area that demands an unprecedented level of coordination between the two countries for the benefit of both. What are your thoughts on this?

LAU: I think it is an excellent proposal. I have developed elsewhere the idea of Japanese direct investment in Chinese electric utilities to facilitate the reduction of acid rain in Japan. The basic idea is as follows: The Chinese electric utilities use predominantly coal-fired power plants—China still relies on coal for 70 percent of its primary energy. As coal is burned, hydrogen sulfide and sulfur dioxide are generated and released into the air. The wind carries these gases across the sea, where they become acid rain and fall onto Korea and Japan, which leads to significant health risks and other damage.

If the coal is scrubbed before its use in the power plants, the sulfur content can be greatly reduced, causing a corresponding reduction in the noxious gases and hence less acid rain. Chinese utilities on their own have little incentive to scrub the coal because it will increase their costs with no corresponding financial benefit. But it may make sense for Japanese investors to own and operate the electric utilities in China with Japanese government subsidies, using scrubbed coal. The increased cost of the scrubbed coal can be more than offset by the savings from not having to clean up and otherwise remediate the damages caused by acid rain in Japan. Thus, the externalities generated by the use of coal by China-based electric utilities can be internalized. As South Korea is also affected by the acid rain resulting from the noxious gases from burning unscrubbed coal, it may also be interested in joining a program investing in clean-coal electric utilities in China.

The Chinese people, especially those who live in the major cities, are now very concerned about the quality of their air and water. I believe China can learn a great deal from the Japanese experience of cleaning up the water in Tokyo Bay and the air quality in Osaka in the 1980s. Chinese energy efficiency in its manufacturing industries lags significantly behind Japan, which has probably achieved the highest energy efficiency in the world, industry by industry. Again, there can be many opportunities for fruitful and mutually beneficial cooperation. Improvement in energy efficiency in the Chinese manufacturing industries will contribute directly to the reduction of carbon emission and the prevention of global climate change.

BILATERAL COORDINATION

LAU: The difference in positions dividing the Chinese and Japanese governments over the sovereignty of the disputed islands is actually quite dangerous.[5] I am sure no one, China, Japan or the United States, wants a war at this time. However, the worry is that a war may be triggered by an unintentional accident that spins out of control.

What we should try to promote are more people-to-people exchanges, especially among our youth. The more the Chinese and Japanese people get to know one another as genuine human beings, the more they will commit to supporting long-term peace and friendship among themselves. Mr. Ikeda, this is exactly where you and your organization can play a leading role.

IKEDA: The Soka Gakkai is currently prioritizing three areas of exchange—among ordinary citizens, among cultures, and among young people.

In 2014, to celebrate the 120th anniversary of the birth of Peking Opera master Mei Lanfang, first president of the China National Peking Opera Company, a delegation from the company was invited on a special tour of Japan by the Min-On Concert Association, which I founded. The performances, which ran from May 14 to July 3 at venues throughout the country, drew rave reviews.

Also in May 2014, a youth delegation from the Soka Gakkai visited China at the invitation of the All-China Youth Federation. The delegates took part in activities promoting goodwill and friendship in such cities as Beijing, Tianjin, and Guangzhou. They also took part in similar events in Hong Kong before returning to Japan.

The exchange program between the Federation and the Soka Gakkai was established based on my proposal and officially launched when Hu Jintao—the president of the ACYF at the time, and later president of the People's Republic of China—signed a formal agreement during his 1985 visit to Japan. Our exchange has continued for nearly thirty years.

During our youth delegation's 2014 visit to China, the Soka Gakkai and ACYF officially agreed to extend our exchange program for another ten years. Our delegates went to great lengths to deepen goodwill with their Chinese hosts, knowing how strained bilateral ties were at this time.

In addition to the launch of an East Asian Fund for Environmental Cooperation, which I described earlier, I want to reinforce my ideas on buttressing a cooperative regional framework addressing the threat of natural disasters. In the SGI peace proposal I issued in January 2014, I highlighted how a foundation for such mechanisms already exists—the ASEAN Regional Forum, comprising the ASEAN countries, the EU, and sixteen other countries, including Japan, China, the United States, Russia, North Korea, and South Korea.[6] ARF has made disaster relief a priority security issue and has in place a framework to regularly discuss ways to improve cooperation.

ARF conducted three disaster relief exercises by 2014 under a system of civilian control and military support, with medical, sanitation, hygiene, and other relevant teams from various countries participating in coordinated drills. Drawing on this ARF experience, I proposed that an Asian recovery resilience agreement be adopted. I called for Japan, China, and South Korea in particular to mutually strengthen resilience initiatives based on existing sister-city agreements between local governments. This would pave the way to establishing a prototypical model promoting cooperative disaster relief efforts on a region-wide basis.

By 2014, there were 354 sister-city agreements between Japan and China, 154 between Japan and South Korea, and 150 between China and South Korea. Given this foundation, I believe we need to forge stronger ties of friendship and trust through collaborative endeavors that fortify resilience, including disaster prevention and mitigation, from the local government level. This initiative would surely add to and improve upon Asia's record of united action and peaceful coexistence that transcend national borders. Such an initiative, together with the need to discuss environmental issues, would justify the holding of a summit among Japan, China, and South Korea, in which national leaders would discuss ways to strengthen cooperation.

I want to add that measures to enhance security in line with this effort should always avert the possibility of a "security dilemma"— a vicious cycle in which any steps a state takes to heighten security are perceived by other states as an increased threat, spurring them to adopt similar measures, which, in turn, fuels further mistrust and tension. In contrast to military-based technologies and resources, the knowledge, information, technology, and know-how in the field of disaster prevention and response are such that their value to all parties is enhanced through sharing. I believe the need to establish an intra-regional framework with which to cope with natural disasters and other challenges is clear, given that Asia has long had to cope with serious risks and damages from earthquakes, typhoons, and abnormal weather events.

Capitalism and Socialism

Ikeda: Let's return to our discussion of the economy. Some people have suggested that the global financial crisis triggered by the implosion of subprime mortgage loans exposed the contradictions of a capitalist economy. Both capitalism, which professes the ideal of freedom, and socialism, which has upheld the ideal of equality, have tried to overcome their shortcomings by, respectively, redistributing wealth through welfare systems and introducing market principles. But with the collapse of socialism, some say capitalism, as the "victorious" economic system, has run amok. What do you think of this view?

Lau: Mr. Ikeda, I think there is some justification for people to say that the fall of socialism resulted in capitalism running rampant. The fall of socialism, as practiced in the former Soviet Union and Eastern Europe, gave people in the developed Western economies false confidence and reinforced the blind faith that the capitalist system can do no wrong.

People claim that government intervention is unnecessary and even harmful, that a completely free market system is the best—the freer the markets, and the less government regulation, the better. The superiority, or the optimality, of the free market system has become an article of faith for many people. But that is what it is—only an article of faith.

People lose sight of the fact that for a market system to deliver the desirable outcomes of economic efficiency and to self-regulate, certain conditions must hold—that the markets are truly competitive, that they allow free entry and exit, that there is no information asymmetry among the market participants, and that there is little room for moral hazard. Otherwise, the markets will fail to deliver economic efficiency, and worse, may lead to asset price bubbles, which have been around for centuries (as examples, the so-called tulipomania, which occurred in the Netherlands in 1637, the property price bubble in Japan in the early 1990s, and the more recent residential housing price bubble in the United States between 1997 and 2006).

IKEDA: I find it particularly disturbing that the financial products resulting from the latest advances in the field had in fact fueled the American asset bubble, eventually triggering the unprecedented financial crisis that began in the United States in 2008. It was a devastating cascade of events. The dangers of creating profits solely through financial manipulation and the reaping of enormous profits have been frequently cited.

Recently, some of the more conscionable members of the business community, lamenting the present situation, are calling for reforms. You have also consistently advocated that participants in a market economy be given fair and equal access to information in an effort to manage moral hazards.

LAU: As I pointed out, the truth is that for a market system to operate properly, some regulation by the government is indispensable. Moreover, a pure market system is ill equipped to correct large inequities in the distribution of income that results from the existing inherited distribution of assets. Redistribution can only be achieved through a separate system of taxation, imposed and enforced by the government.

IKEDA: China has emerged as a vital player in both Asia and the world as a result of the striking economic advances it achieved after adopting a market economy within the context of a socialist system. It has been as much an epic challenge as it has been a remarkable feat.

In your opinion, what kind of policies must China adopt going forward?

LAU: The success of Chinese economic reform and opening to the world since 1978 is due, in part, to the introduction of elements of capitalism into the Chinese economy—free markets, profit maximization, and monetary incentives. However, as I noted, the market system itself cannot and does not redistribute income. To achieve a fair and equitable but not necessarily egalitarian distribution of personal income, government intervention in the form of taxation and transfer payment policies is necessary.

The current economic goal of the Chinese Communist Party is to assure the achievement of a moderate level of prosperity for the entire country by 2020. The definition of a "moderate level of prosperity" adopted by the party is for all citizens to have comprehensive medical and social insurance, to have their own residences, and for no citizen to live under the poverty line.[7]

I believe this is achievable, but as you can see, the government must play a leading role in making this possible. Even in a wealthy economy such as the United States, until recently, approximately 20 percent of its citizens were without health insurance.

Distribution and redistribution of income are also important functions of an economic system. In a capitalist market economy, distribution is in accordance with the marginal product of one's labor, as well as the marginal product of the capital owned. But this distribution depends on the initial distribution of capital, both human and physical. Thus, redistribution may become necessary.

In a socialist economy, the distribution formula becomes "From each according to his ability, to each according to his work (labor investment)." Ultimately, this is supposed to progress to "From each according to his ability, to each according to his need," when there is abundance and communism is achieved. But it may prove to be a utopian ideal that can never be truly realized.

CONVERSATION SEVEN

Learning As Growth

IKEDA: Learning is the light; it empowers people, leading them to joy and triumphant lives. Professor Lau, you have taught your students that the most valuable gift a university can bestow isn't only a diploma or academic degree but also the lifelong ability to learn for themselves. You are a firm believer that education's primary objective should be to cultivate the process of learning rather than the mere acquisition of knowledge. I agree with you that this is an invaluable point.

Makiguchi shared a similar view:

> The aim of education is not to transfer knowledge; it is to guide the learning process, to put the responsibility for study into the students' own hands. It is not the piecemeal merchandising of information; it [also] is the provision of keys that will allow people to unlock the vault of knowledge on their own.[1]

LAU: I'm honored to learn that Mr. Makiguchi had this perspective on education: We share the same ideals.

IKEDA: In your opinion, what should higher education do to assist students in developing their ability to learn on their own?

LAU: Teaching students how to learn on their own or apply this learning process is no simple task. It is something that students gradually assimilate over time as they interact with teachers who consistently serve as models to emulate. Thus, the learning process can only be taught and acquired through an interactive teacher-student relationship.

Universities should encourage students to engage in research— voluntary or mandatory—from an early phase in their studies in order for them to acquire the requisite self-learning skills. That is why I believe the Internet, which offers an immense range of knowledge at the touch of a finger, possesses such remarkable potential.

IKEDA: These self-learning skills, then, will serve as the basis with which to lead a better life.

Shortly before his death, Lu Xun reportedly said that he would strive to learn as long as he lived.[2] Indeed, a person who continues to do so over a lifetime becomes truly human. Or perhaps we could even say that one of the main purposes of life itself is to learn.

I believe it is especially important for us, in order to forge our character and deepen our humanity, to study and master the way of learning through a relationship with someone we hold as a mentor in life.

I think it could also be said that you, yourself, experienced this as a student at Stanford, where you met a professor who dramatically transformed your life. I would therefore like to ask you about your student days in the United States. You earned top grades at Stanford and graduated one year early, after just three years of study.

LAU: I cannot say that I studied very hard when I was an undergraduate student at Stanford, except for the very first quarter. I did all the work required, but I must confess that I did not necessarily attend all the classes. For some courses, such as introductory economics, philosophy, and political science, I had a 100 percent attendance record, taking a seat in the front row, completely captivated by the teachers. For others, my attendance record was spottier. For this reason, I never feel it is appropriate for me to take roll call in the classes I teach or penalize any student for not attending my class—as long as a student does all the required work, including taking the required examinations.

I did take a heavy course load—there was one quarter in my sophomore year in which I took twenty-six units (compared to a typical fifteen units), and I also passed some courses just by taking the required tests and examinations. So ultimately, I was able to graduate from Stanford University after three years instead of the normal four years.

IKEDA: So your emphasis on the independence and initiative of students stems from that time. US universities, I have heard, emphasize performance, which promotes students' intellectual growth but at the same time can be very demanding. Foreigners who have come to study in a host country have the additional hurdles of language and culture to overcome.

It is widely perceived that few Japanese students have a desire to study overseas. While there are a variety of reasons for this—lack of confidence in foreign languages, the financial burden, and greater difficulty in finding work upon returning to Japan—a number of measures are being fast-tracked by the government and other parties to remedy the situation. I believe further steps should be taken sooner rather than later.

EXCHANGE STUDENTS

IKEDA: I'm sure you have many memories of your studies in the United States, but what was one of the most challenging or difficult situations you faced?

We have many international students at both Soka University of America and Soka University of Japan. In a ranking of "Best Colleges of 2014," the *US News & World Report* ranked SUA first among all US liberal arts colleges in both its "foreign student factor"—the ratio of non-US students enrolled[3]—and percentage of students—100 percent—who engage in study abroad programs while enrolled at the university.[4]

I wonder if you could provide, based on your experience, any encouragement or advice for students studying away from their home countries.

LAU: As you suggest, the most difficult part of my student days at Stanford was to adjust to living in a different cultural environment. While studying there in 1961, there was no other freshman student from Hong Kong, Taiwan, or mainland China. I did not speak a word of Chinese during the first quarter I was at Stanford.

There were also many different usages between British and American English, in addition to the different pronunciation and spelling that I had to learn and adopt, such as "elevator" for "lift," "eraser" for "rubber," "hood" for "bonnet," and "trunk" for "boot." However, the American students were generally very friendly and made me feel quite at home. And the Foreign Student Advisor's Office was also most helpful.

I made many friends as an undergraduate student at Stanford. My advice to foreign students everywhere is that they should make maximum use of the time they spend in the host country— they should not be shy but should approach and seek out local students, maintaining an open attitude, so that they can learn about their culture, values, and society, however different they may appear. Of course, it is important to have some prior fluency in the local language, otherwise the benefits of overseas study cannot be fully realized.

IKEDA: When one can proactively interact with people of one's host country and learn from its culture and various customs, this is likely to instill the ability to view things from a broader perspective and nurture a more tolerant attitude toward different cultures and values. Indeed, I'm convinced that the experience serves as fertile ground in creating the broadmindedness required of a global citizen.

In a speech you gave when you became vice chancellor of CUHK, you said:

> Our non-local students will become part of our intangible capital. If they return to their respective home countries or regions, they become part of our durable network of friends and goodwill ambassadors. By opening up opportunities here for others, we in turn also open up opportunities for ourselves elsewhere.[5]

I'm happy to report that Soka University students who have studied at CUHK have been warmly welcomed and, upon diligently tackling their studies there, have become better individuals for the experience. Among them are students who have since become faculty members at our university and are now providing Chinese language instruction, while others have contributed significantly to advancing exchange between Japan, Hong Kong, and China. I also hear regularly of the achievements of exchange students from CUHK who have studied at Soka University.

Such students are indispensable in bringing countries closer together, and they should emerge as future leaders. Like you, I engage our students from abroad with this belief firmly in mind.

Soka University was the first Japanese university to officially accept students from the People's Republic of China in 1975 after bilateral ties were restored. When we accepted the first students, I personally acted as their guarantor. Whenever I visited the university, I met with them and asked what problems or concerns they might have as they strove to acclimate themselves to life in Japan, encouraging them to speak frankly. I even worked up a sweat playing in a table-tennis tournament that our university organized to deepen our friendship with them.

Today, of those first six students from China, several serve as ranking envoys in China's diplomatic corps, while others have become leading contributors to international exchange. As Soka University founder, nothing could make me happier.

During your time as a Stanford University student, what were your impressions of America, the "land of the free"? I'm sure you were anxious about some things, but you equally must have had high expectations.

AMERICA IN THE 1960S

LAU: I went to the United States in 1961. It coincided with the beginning of a period of significant political and social change there.

In the 1950s, with the gradual decline of the power and influence of the United Kingdom and France, and the rise of the Soviet Union—as was manifested in its successful nuclear tests and launch of the Sputnik, the first man-made satellite—the United States became the undisputed leader of the free world.

A youthful John F. Kennedy was elected US president in 1960, projecting a progressive and forward-looking image. Unfortunately, President Kennedy was assassinated in 1963.

He was succeeded by Lyndon B. Johnson. President Johnson managed to persuade the US Congress to pass the 1964 Civil Rights Act, under which the legal rights of African-Americans are protected through and by the federal government. This was a most important piece of legislation.

Despite the fact that the Civil War ended in 1865 with the Union side in victory, the black minority did not actually enjoy equal rights, though they might have existed on paper, until 1964. Racial segregation had remained intact—in housing, in schools, in transportation, in voting, even in restaurants—in many Southern states and in some Northern states at the time.

IKEDA: August 2013 marked the fiftieth anniversary of the March on Washington for Jobs and Freedom, during which Dr. Martin Luther King Jr. gave his famous "I Have a Dream" speech. I have engaged in discussions with Dr. Vincent Harding, a close friend and fellow activist of King, on the history and spirit of the civil rights movement. I also have fond memories of meeting, in both the United States and Japan, with the activist Rosa Parks, who played a central role in the Montgomery bus boycott.

As I understand, following the end of the Civil War, Congress passed the Civil Rights Acts of 1866 and 1875, making it illegal to discriminate against African-Americans in public places, including on public transportation and in hotels. In the South, however, numerous discriminatory statutes—the so-called Jim Crow laws—were subsequently enacted, legalizing various forms of racial discrimination.

As Dr. Harding explained to me:

> When I share the story of the civil rights movement, I have to tell about the long, and often cruel, bloodstained history that led up to it. Yet it is impossible to adequately convey the fears and apprehensions of black people in the last decades of the nineteenth century, many of whom

worried—even after the abolition of slavery and the ratifi-
cation of the Thirteenth Amendment to the U.S. Constitution—that the return of slavery remained a possibility.[6]

Dr. Harding went on to say, "Black people living in the South
struggled long after the abolition of slavery to be truly free."[7] It
was a prolonged, arduous struggle that defies imagination, one in
which many people, including SGI members in America, their kin
and close friends, took part.

LAU: The passage of the Civil Rights Act of 1964 had a profound
impact on US politics. It effectively ended the coalition between
Northern Democrats, who were mostly liberal, and Southern
Democrats, who were mostly conservative but had remained
Democrats for historical reasons—because President Abraham
Lincoln, who led the Union to victory over the Confederacy, was
a Republican. The Southern Democrats, as well as the Southern
states, gradually all turned Republican. And the situation per-
sisted till today.

Despite this historical legacy, in my opinion, the United States
is still more hospitable and welcoming toward foreigners than any
other country in the world. I was readily accepted. And there is
much less hierarchy and protocol and much more social mobility
in America. People then and now address one another by their
first names. And there is genuine freedom of speech and equality
before the law and, by and large, genuine respect for the rule of law.

Back in the 1960s, racial discrimination was common. In the
summer of 1962, I had a summer job in Anaheim, near Los Ange-
les. I tried to find an apartment to rent, and often it would be
available on the telephone, but when I arrived and saw the land-
lord face to face, I would be told that the apartment was no longer
available.

And people who had to travel between New York and Washington, D.C., at the time remember that the buses, restaurants, and hotels along the way were all racially segregated. An Asian traveling in those days would actually find it difficult and embarrassing to have to figure out where one belonged—white or colored. Fortunately, this is history now.

IKEDA: The election of President Barack Obama symbolizes the immense changes that have taken place in the United States since that time. Speaking of President Obama, Dr. Harding shared this insight:

> Mr. Obama understands that he is an heir to the legacy of King and the movement. He has reminded people that the civil rights movement did not end with King's assassination, nor did it end with the legal recognition of the rights of black people. He has also reminded people that forming a "more perfect Union" is an ongoing endeavor to which we all must commit ourselves for our entire lives and for the life of this nation.[8]

The civil rights movement was and is a struggle for a democracy in which all may lead the lives to which they are entitled as human beings. It continues to be an endless struggle for freedom, equality, justice, and the triumph of humanity that must be advanced by subsequent generations.

DIVORCED FROM REALITY

IKEDA: To return to an earlier subject, I am astonished that you earned your degree as a foreign student at one of America's top universities in just three years. And on top of that, you concurrently earned degrees in two fields, physics and economics. Why did you decide to major in two such different areas of study concurrently?

LAU: Actually, I started out with a major in engineering. After a couple quarters as an engineering major, I discovered that I really did not like to do engineering drawings, so I switched my major to physics. This was the flexibility of the US tertiary educational system, which allowed students to change majors easily without losing any time.

I knew nothing about economics then, but Stanford required that every undergraduate student take at least two subjects in social sciences, and I selected economics and political science. In the third quarter of my freshman year, I took Economics 1, Introduction to Economics, from Professor John G. Gurley, using the textbook *Economics* by Paul A. Samuelson. Professor Gurley was such a great teacher, and the book by Samuelson was so captivating, that I decided to double major in physics and economics.

In my last undergraduate year at Stanford, I began to feel that physics was also becoming too abstract and unreal, looking at particles so minute that no one could ever really see them. I thought economics dealt with much more concrete, real-world phenomena. That is why I decided to pursue graduate study in economics.

I did not realize until much later that there are branches of economics that could be even more abstract and divorced from reality than physics. However, I have no regrets about choosing economics over physics. Ultimately, I believe I am more suited for doing something that can help people more directly.

IKEDA: "Help people more directly"—this certainly articulates your beliefs as clearly as it does your passion for scholarship.

I am surprised to learn that, at the start, you weren't majoring in either physics or economics.

The challenge, I suppose, lies in how one correlates university education with social realities. This is why I was interested to hear from you about CUHK's rich educational environment, which you helped establish during your tenure as vice chancellor. Your university, for example, organizes lectures by Nobel Prize winners and distinguished speakers from various sectors of society and holds simultaneous broadcasts of these lectures with Peking University.

As you have stated: "It is extremely important that students understand how society actually functions. Therefore, it is essential that they learn not only theory, but also be exposed to practical experience."[9]

You also offered this observation:

> We must always remember that knowledge is not only deductive in nature, but that it emerges from inductive processes as well. Even if a plan looks great on paper, it often may not be feasible. This is why I believe that inviting to the university speakers from outside of academia who are prominent in their fields is an indispensable means of helping students gain an accurate and balanced perspective of the world.[10]

You raise an invaluable point. As a rule, reality rarely follows theory; it is only by recognizing what is real that we can develop more elaborate theories and apply them.

Toda firmly believed in grasping a situation firsthand and perceiving the true nature of the issues unique to each situation to come up with the best solutions. He thus made sure that I was assigned to the most challenging posts, be it at work or within the Soka Gakkai.

He would often tell me, "Learn from the best." When you come to know people exceptional at what they do, it broadens your perspectives and is sure to prove stimulating.

Which is why Soka University of Japan holds a lecture series called "Leaders in Contemporary Management" featuring, among others, presidents and chairs of various companies. We also invite leaders, academics, literary figures, and artists of the world to visit Soka University, Soka Women's College, and the Soka schools.

Asked their impressions after these lectures, our students seem to have astutely grasped what these distinguished individuals share: They all possess illuminating insights on life; they are well educated and deeply humane; and they are committed to contributing to social betterment in one form or another—despite being experts in varying fields. As the German writer Johann Wolfgang von Goethe said, "Young people prefer inspiration to instruction."[11] These encounters with the most successful men and women in their fields have proven to be priceless opportunities for students, inspiring them greatly.

ECONOMICS AND PHYSICS

IKEDA: Interdisciplinary research, in which scholars of different fields cooperate, has become increasingly important. One such discipline is econophysics, which is attracting attention recently. What points in common do physics and economics have?

LAU: It turns out that many economists, including Professor Paul A. Samuelson, started out as physicists. One common feature of physics and economics is the reliance on both theoretical analysis and empirical research. Empirical research is meant to confirm or refute theoretical analysis. In turn, empirical research may generate results that provide inspiration and stimulation for new theoretical analysis.

They are both different from mathematics, because both physics and economics have to interface with the real world. Ultimately, they must be able to develop theoretical models that are capable of explaining real phenomena. Thus, the study of physics is actually good preparation for the study of economics.

However, physics and economics also differ in one important

respect: While one can conduct controlled experiments in physics to test a theoretical model, no controlled experiments are possible in economics—one has to take the empirical observations on the economy as they actually occur. This difference has led to different methodologies for the analysis of the observed data of physics and economics. Actually, economics is more comparable to astrophysics, a field in which controlled experiments are not possible, and observations have to be made under natural conditions.

IKEDA: It's fascinating that economics resembles astrophysics in that controlled experiments to test theoretical models are not possible. I would assume that this is also an indication of the difficulty of making economic predictions.

You mentioned Professor Samuelson earlier. His *Economics* is used as a text book for modern economics around the world to this day. When you were studying in the United States in the 1960s, American society was prospering as a result of the postwar economic boom, and I'm told that the economics proposed by Professor Samuelson and others provided theoretical backing for that growth.

At the same time, the domestic economy was taking a turn for the worse, while military spending mushroomed because of escalating US involvement in the Vietnam War. This was compounded by the failure of various welfare and unemployment policies instituted to combat poverty under the "Great Society" program put forward by President Lyndon B. Johnson, who succeeded President Kennedy after his assassination. It was during this period that you made outstanding achievements in your chosen field of economics.

During your graduate program at Berkeley, you were hired for a teaching position at Stanford. At about what time did you begin to focus on the Chinese economy?

LAU: My return to Stanford as an acting assistant professor in 1966 was quite serendipitous. I was twenty-one years old then, happily enjoying my second year of graduate study at Berkeley. I had no clear idea what I was getting into, but the salary offered by Stanford was much better than my fellowship at Berkeley, and no teaching duties for the first year sounded good, so I accepted. Thus began my long teaching career of forty years at Stanford, until my formal retirement there in 2006.

I was originally hired by Stanford specifically to teach and to conduct research on the Chinese economy. While I did construct the first econometric model of mainland China in 1966, I did not really focus on the Chinese economy until much later, when China began its economic reform and opened up to the world in 1978. And a year later, I had the opportunity to visit mainland China for the first time as an adult.

IKEDA: Ever since China adopted a policy of economic reform and liberalization, the Chinese economy has averaged real GDP growth of around 10 percent annually. And it continues to grow today as the world's second largest economy.

By the way, John Kenneth Galbraith is known as one of the first to foresee Japan's rapid postwar economic development. In a January 1, 2005, interview with the *Mainichi Shimbun*, one of Japan's leading daily newspapers, he described Japan's economic growth as an undeniable "success story" yet added that the situation had changed with the emergence of China in the world economy and the future potential of India. He cautioned that Japan faces increasingly stiff competition from other countries in Asia, and that should matters progress over the next decade as they have over the previous decade, China will be the center of world attention, and Japan will be left in its shadow.

Sometime before he made these comments, Dr. Galbraith told me that he was certain that China and India were well on their way to becoming economic successes. He pointed out that the longstanding divisions between capitalism and socialism would disappear when discussing the dizzying changes taking place in the global economy, and that capitalism in its traditional sense had outlived its day. China's economic development is indeed a prime example of the inapplicability of the traditional categorizations of capitalism and socialism.

CHINA's ECONOMIC DEVELOPMENT

IKEDA: Since 2005, China adopted the goal of maintaining annual GDP growth in the 8-percentile range and has seen its economy rocket forward. While growth had tapered from 2009 in the wake of the global economic crisis following the Lehman Brothers collapse, real GDP in the April–June quarter of 2014 grew by 7.5 percent year-on-year, the first gain in three quarters, according to China's National Bureau of Statistics. In this regard, let me ask your views on the growth of the Chinese economy and its prospects for growth over the next few years.

LAU: The Chinese economy has done well ever since it began its economic reform and opened to the world under Deng Xiaoping in 1978. It has achieved an average annual real rate of growth of almost 10 percent over the past thirty-five years to become the second largest economy in the world, after the United States. It acceded to the World Trade Organization and has now become the second largest trading nation in the world.

However, the Chinese per capita GDP has remained relatively low, at approximately $6,850 in 2013 prices. The real question of interest to everyone is: Can this rate of economic growth be sustained?

The short answer is that an average annual real rate of growth of almost 10 percent cannot be sustained. In fact, the Chinese economy has now reached a stage at which it must begin to change its model of development—from that oriented to exports to that oriented to domestic demand, and driven by innovation rather than inputs. My own forecast is that China will make the adjustments gradually but successfully, and that for the next decade or two, the Chinese economy should be able to grow at an average annual real rate of 7 percent. At this reduced rate of growth of 7 percent, the Chinese economy should almost double itself in ten years and should catch up to the real output of the US economy a year or two before 2030.

Am I too optimistic? I do not believe so. I have been observing the Chinese economy since 1966, when I built my econometric model of China. The factors that support a continuing high rate of growth include, first, the high national saving rate of China of more than 40 percent, which would also enable a continuing high investment rate; second, continuing abundance of surplus labor, especially if one takes into account that the current retirement ages of sixty for men and fifty-five for women in China can and should be raised; and third, a huge domestic market, which would allow significant economies of scale to be realized without reliance on exports. Moreover, China has been stepping up its investments in such intangible capital as human capital (education) and R&D capital.

IKEDA: Having followed developments in China closely for many years, you believe her great economic experiment is proceeding well. According to your analysis, China—given its immense reserves of untapped potential—will continue to enjoy sustainable economic growth in the years to come by expanding domestic consumption and focusing on technological innovation.

LAU: One can gain further insight on Chinese economic growth by applying the "flying geese paradigm" of East Asian economic growth first introduced by Professor Kaname Akamatsu. Basically, just as industrialization spread from economy to economy in East Asia—from Japan to Hong Kong to Taiwan and to South Korea and then to Southeast Asia and to an opening China—industrialization will spread from the Chinese coastal provinces, municipalities, and regions, such as Guangdong, Shanghai, Zhejiang, and Beijing, to the interior provinces of Shaanxi, Sichuan, and Chongqing.

Thus, while the rates of growth of the leading provinces, which used to be in the double digits, will begin to fall, the rates of growth of the lagging provinces will begin to rise. Overall, an average annual rate of growth of 7 percent for the entire country can be maintained.

For many years, most of the Western media have popularized the notion that the Chinese economy must grow at a minimum of 8 percent per annum or there would be social chaos. However, there is no real theoretical analysis or empirical evidence to support this hypothesis.

I believe China can easily survive a decline in the rate of economic growth to even 4 percent for a year or two, although I do not believe it is at all likely. We should bear in mind that even a growth of 4 percent of Chinese GDP today represents the same increase in output as a growth of 8 percent ten years ago.

CONVERSATION EIGHT

Economics for Happiness

IKEDA: Because the economy is vital to both the individual and society, people are quick to criticize and question its efficacy.

Responding concisely to my question about what kind of twenty-first century he wanted to see, Galbraith said that he hoped it would be an age in which people found life in this world to be a joy and a time when killing had come to an end. Galbraith lived through two world wars and believed strongly that we must not allow war to break out again. He insisted that politics, economics, and science were basically means to advance the welfare and wellbeing of humanity, but because modern society had lost sight of this, these fields had instead become ends in themselves.

I was struck by his forthright, astute belief that economics must serve human happiness. However, while many acknowledge that the study of economics is important, there are some who find the discipline complex and difficult to understand. How would you describe the workings of an economy in modern society?

LAU: In a country or region, an economy is a system for the determination of, first, the assignment of the primary factors of production, including capital, labor, and natural resources, to enterprises and organizations, including governmental organizations and their compensation; second, the type and quantity of goods and services, including capital and consumer goods and services, that are to be produced by these enterprises and organizations, and the pricing of these goods and services; and third, the distribution of these goods and services to the different enterprises, organizations, and households for use as intermediate inputs or to be consumed. Whether an economy is a centrally planned one, a market one, or a mixed one, it must fulfill these necessary basic functions.

In addition, the government is responsible for the financing (through taxes and the issuance of public debt, if necessary) and provision of public goods, such as education, health care, national defense, public security (including firefighting and police protection), and public infrastructure. The government also has the responsibility for the stabilization of the economy (to smooth out the cyclical fluctuations of the economy and to control inflation), the promotion of full employment, and the support of sustainable long-term economic growth.

Further, the government is responsible for the redistribution of income through income taxes and transfer payments, so that the gains of economic prosperity can be better shared by all. The provision of public goods, such as education, medical care, environmental preservation, pollution control, and public parks, by the government can be a very effective "in kind" redistribution mechanism.

IKEDA: Thank you for clarifying the relationship between economic activity and government. Governance is truly a skilled craft. The challenge of politics lies in balancing economic growth with enhancing the quality of people's lives and ensuring that this effort is stable and sustainable.

Toda often told us that individual happiness should never be sacrificed at the altar of social prosperity, rather the two must advance hand in hand. I believe there is a growing urgency for economic activity to not only focus on efficiency but also the greater public good.

LAU: Yes. Allow me to add that to an economist, efficiency has a very specific meaning—a state of the economy such that the output of any good or service cannot be increased without decreasing the output of another good or service. Efficiency, in laymen's terms, simply means that all resources are being put to their highest and best use, and that no resource is wasted.

The efficient use of resources includes the use of human resources. Sun Yat-sen, in a petition he submitted to Li Hongzhang, viceroy of Zhili, in 1894, described a vision of an efficient economy, in which every person would be able to use his talent to the fullest, every piece of land would be exploited to its highest benefit, everything would realize its maximum usefulness, and every good would be able to move freely (to where it was most needed).

But such a state of affairs cannot be obtained automatically. A free market system cannot achieve efficiency by itself. Only a truly competitive market system, satisfying certain conditions, can result in an efficient economy.

This is where the government must come in—to regulate and supervise the operations of the market system, so that it becomes and remains truly competitive. In certain markets in which natural monopolies prevail, such as electricity generation and distribution, more direct regulation and supervision may be required. For example, in many developed market economies, public utilities are regulated by public utility commissions, which have the power to approve or disapprove any proposed price change, if the utilities are not owned, managed, and operated by a government corporation directly.

IKEDA: Yes, this is a vital role the government fulfills. If I remember correctly, you have often said that economic trends have their unique rules and patterns.

LAU: One idea that has broad applications in many different settings is the hypothesis of "self-fulfilling expectations." It highlights the important role that collective expectations play in an economy.

A few years back, Japan was in a deep recession. Many households and firms expected that it would be worse the next year, and so they each independently decided to cut back on their respective consumption and investment. And because of this cutback, the next year did turn out to be worse. So the expectations were fulfilled, actually self-fulfilled.

IKEDA: This means it is equally possible for widespread expectations to *drive* economic growth.

LAU: The Chinese economic boom in 1992 following the southern visit[1] of Deng Xiaoping was another example of "self-fulfilling expectations." The Chinese economy then was dead in the water in the aftermath of the Tiananmen Square protests of 1989.[2] After the Deng visit, everyone thought the economy was going to boom and acted accordingly, and the result was a huge boom.

However, not all expectations are self-fulfilling. There are also "self non-fulfilling expectations." For example, with the debut of a new and exciting movie, everyone might expect that all the tickets would have been sold out and hence decide not to go to see the movie. The end result might be a half-empty theater.

IKEDA: I am reminded again just how difficult it is to predict economic trends. Obviously, operating any business would be a simple matter if people could accurately forecast the future.

As Galbraith said, the fundamental force that drives an economy is people. No matter how trying our plight may be or how daunting the adversity we face, he was convinced that as long as human beings remain strong and resilient, then we would forge on, reversing our fortunes and recovering to the point that we would once again leap ahead and eventually create a truly prosperous society.[3]

As you may know, Galbraith advised President Franklin D. Roosevelt on economic policy as the latter strove to rebuild the American economy in the years following the Great Depression. Galbraith shared with me a famous passage from Roosevelt's 1933 inaugural address, in which the newly elected president called out to his fellow Americans, whose spirits had nearly been broken by years of economic distress: "First of all, let me assert my firm belief that the only thing we have to fear is fear itself—nameless, unreasoning, unjustified terror which paralyzes needed efforts to convert retreat into advance."[4] This is a classic illustration of just how valuable good leadership is in times of crisis.

YOUTH EMPLOYMENT

IKEDA: In Japan today, young Japanese are finding it difficult to hope for a better future—which comes as no surprise, given the number of jobless youth, the expansion of nonpermanent or irregular employment, the growing number of the working poor, and other uncertainties they face.

How does this compare with Hong Kong?

LAU: Hong Kong faces many of the same problems. Many young people are not optimistic about their future prospects.

Part of the problem arises from the gradual disappearance of well-paying jobs. Manufacturing jobs have largely disappeared from Hong Kong, to either mainland China or to Southeast Asia, a result of the rising degree of globalization. (Automation and robotics have not yet affected Hong Kong but have had a significant impact in the United States.)

The advancement in information and communication technologies has also caused many middle-level managerial positions to become redundant, as the span of control of senior management expands, and the organization of an enterprise becomes flatter and flatter.

For example, in a commercial bank, there used to be layers of middle management between the president and the tellers—not anymore. It is possible for a single senior vice president to monitor the work of a thousand lower-level employees. The same information and communication revolution has also enabled even the back-office jobs to move away to lower-cost locations elsewhere. The result is a diminution of advancement of opportunities and rising disparity in the distribution of income.

What can be done about these problems? They are not easy to solve in the short run. I have advocated for Hong Kong and elsewhere to create jobs that cannot be moved away—for example, jobs in the tourism industry and in industries that cater to tourists. However, these are by and large low-paying jobs. If young people are to aspire to greater opportunities, they should consider going north.

Just as the ambitious young Americans responded to the call of "Go West, young man!" in the nineteenth century, the young people of Hong Kong should do the same; they should venture into the mainland, the land of opportunities and, of course, of risks. But if there is no risk, there can be no gain; if one does not take some risks when one is young, when will one take risks?

IKEDA: Young people should indeed dare to tackle ambitious goals.

This is somewhat of an aside, but I clearly recall Toda offering the following advice to a young man troubled by what career he should pursue:

> There are three standards when choosing a job. They are the values of beauty, benefit, and good. Everyone would ideally like to find the kind of work they like (beauty), is profitable (benefit), and contributes to the betterment of society (good). The real world, however, is not as accommodating as you'd believe. In fact, only a handful of people are likely to find that perfect job they hoped to land from the very beginning. More often than not, people are forced to work at a job they never expected to do.

Granted, a person may land a job he or she enjoys but doesn't pay enough (beauty without benefit) or may be working for the welfare of others yet may not like the job (good without beauty) and so on. Thus, it is quite rare in reality to find work in which the three values of beauty, benefit, and good coincide.

Should the young man become mired in less-than favorable employment, Toda counseled:

> It is essential that you work with all your might at your present job, that you become someone who is truly indispensable to your employer and fellow workers. And by soldiering on, you will definitely be able to work at a job you like, one that is profitable and contributes to society in a significant manner. That is the power and proof of faith. All the hard work you put in will not be wasted and that experience will remain a cherished asset throughout your life. One day, you'll realize that everything you had to undergo served a purpose. I can say this without equivocation from my own experience.

Having seen countless other individuals with similar experiences, I feel deep in my heart the veracity of Toda's words.

LAU: That's very instructive advice. I have often advised the students at the Chinese University of Hong Kong on their career choice, "Do what you love, and love what you do!"

IKEDA: Clearly, governments should assign employment among their highest priorities and tackle the issue accordingly. The dearth of jobs and work opportunities not only forces the unemployed into dire economic straits but makes them feel useless and unneeded, deepening their sense of alienation and, in some cases, sapping their lives of hope.

The International Labour Organisation has been urging countries to secure what it describes as "decent work" for citizens. According to the ILO report "Global Employment Trends 2014," some 74.5 million young people ages 15–24 remained jobless in 2013.[5] This is a serious situation requiring immediate redress.

Dr. M. S. Swaminathan, the agricultural geneticist and former president of the Pugwash Conferences on Science and World Affairs, has been a consistent advocate of and agent for solutions to remedy global poverty and the food crisis as well as widespread unemployment. In September 2013, he spoke at a peace seminar held at the University of Madras in India, an event co-organized by the university, the M. S. Swaminathan Research Foundation, and Bharat (India) Soka Gakkai. Dr. Swaminathan mentioned the peace proposal I issued in 2013.[6] In the proposal, I called for all nations to implement a "Social Protection Floor" ensuring that those suffering from extreme poverty can regain a sense of dignity. I further cited estimates by the relevant UN agencies that it should be possible for countries at every stage of economic development to cover the necessary costs for minimum income and livelihood guarantees—and the news that some thirty developing countries have already begun implementing such plans. Dr. Swaminathan shared that in order to aid the impoverished and advance social betterment, there exists an urgent need to provide them with proper healthcare and education in addition to adequate food.

In one of the discussions we shared, Dr. Swaminathan explained that it was equally vital to develop initiatives that secure jobs for those in less fortunate circumstances, enabling them to earn an income and decent housing. He pointed out the tremendous imbalance of wealth in the world, with the five wealthiest countries having a greater GNP than the next fifty nations combined. With the majority of the world living in abject poverty, it was imperative, he said, that we provide all people a quality of life allowing them to lead truly human lives. We need to reorient ourselves from a profit-driven economy to an economy that values the dignity of human life, he concluded. I also believe humanity can no longer avoid confronting these challenges.

The Emerging BRICS

IKEDA: I want now to turn to Makiguchi. As an educator and geographer, he wrote at age thirty-two a major work titled *Jinsei chirigaku* (A Geography of Human Life), in which he discussed the interrelationship between human life and nature.

In this work, he also offered a unique perspective on the state and the market. Makiguchi suggested a way of looking at the nation-state as a business, a commercial operation. In other words, as distances shrink, and time is compressed in the modernizing world, the entire planet becomes one vast market of supply and demand. From one point of view, Japan may appear to be facing off against the rest of the world, but from the perspective of economics, it is fully integrated into this great global market, just one "shop" among many, as it were, assigned a particular function for the cooperative advancement of human life as a whole, selling its output as one part of what is produced globally.[7]

Jinsei chirigaku was published in 1903, the year before the Russo-Japanese War broke out. Though it was a period of increasing imperialism, Makiguchi had already recognized that Japan was but one nation among many and grasped the appropriate role it should play.

Today, as globalization marches on at an accelerating pace, the world's countries are even more closely interconnected. For better or worse, they exert a powerful influence on one another and have inevitably come to compete with one another on a global basis.

What country or countries do you believe will assume an important position in the world in the foreseeable future for reasons not limited to their economic role?

Lau: There has been a great deal of talk about the rise of the BRICS countries (Brazil, Russia, India, China, and South Africa). I have already covered China. Let me talk about the others in turn.

Brazil has a population of 200 million, the sixth largest in the world. It has a GDP of US$2.5 trillion. Its per capita GDP is in excess of $10,000 per person.

However, Brazil's economic growth record is a little erratic. The Brazilian economy will go through a decade or so of rapid growth, only to run into bottlenecks or balance-of-payments problems.

The fundamental problem is its low national saving rate, which makes it overly reliant on the inflow of foreign direct investment and foreign loans. But foreign capital is often short-term and fickle. When it is withdrawn at the first sign of trouble, the Brazilian economy will run into problems. However, with the largest population in Latin America and a rich base of natural resources, Brazil is potentially an important player on the world scene.

Russia is already an important country because of its military might and because of its large oil and gas reserves. It currently has a population in excess of 140 million and a GDP of $2 trillion, the eighth largest GDP in the world. Russian military power is second only to that of the United States, and the Russian economy is doing fine thanks to its oil and gas production. Russia will continue to play an important role in the world.

I believe India will rise to become an important world power. It currently has a population of 1.2 billion, the second largest in the world, just after China. India is likely, in the next couple decades, to surpass China as the most populous nation in the world. The Indian economy, with its huge labor force, almost universal basic education, and vast internal market, is very much like China before its economic reform and opening to the world in 1978. With the appropriate economic reform policies, there is no reason why India cannot achieve the same successful growth as China.

India has the additional advantage that English is the common language used by all educated Indians. There are also many expatriate Indians around the world who can contribute to India's economic development.

If genuine peace can take hold in South Asia, which includes Bangladesh, Pakistan, and Sri Lanka, there is no limit to the economic potential of the Indian subcontinent. A South Asian Free Trade Area will have a population of more than 1.6 billion, larger than that of China. Bangladesh has been booming economically. Why not India?

South Africa, based on its abundant natural resources, has significant upside potential, but it must try to industrialize through the development of manufacturing. It currently has a population of 50 million and a GDP of $400 billion. Its per capita GDP is slightly higher than that of China.

South Africa and perhaps Nigeria, too, can become major

players in Africa eventually. However, I believe the major challenges there are how to achieve a social consensus and how to realize effective governance.

Among other East Asian countries, Indonesia also has the potential to assume an important position in its region.

What should be emphasized in all of these economies is the development of the manufacturing sector. At their existing stages of development, only the expansion of the manufacturing sector can provide a sufficient number of jobs that can lead to rising incomes and skills over time.

IKEDA: That's a concise and instructive overview, Professor Lau. I understand that the BRICS countries have been the focus of great interest as emerging economies in recent years. These five countries represent roughly 40 percent of the world's population and some 20 percent of its GDP as of 2013.[8] India is expected to become the world's most populous nation, projected to reach 1.45 billion people by 2028.

In a speech I gave in October 1997 at the Rajiv Gandhi Institute for Contemporary Studies in India, I posited that three countries—China, the United States, and India—would play central roles in the twenty-first century, and that three great powers would enhance stability rather than just two. I said that a world dominated by two great powers inevitably tends toward conflict, whereas three can open the way for dialogue and solidarity, moving the entire world toward peace.

India, I said, was poised to make a dramatic leap into the twenty-first century, impelled by a market economy and advanced technology. And given its profound spiritual tradition, India's message of nonviolence is of paramount significance.

Needless to say, Brazil and the other BRICS countries are similarly endowed in terms of their splendid spirituality and culture. Let me add that we have SGI members in Brazil, Russia, India, and South Africa striving to better their respective communities and countries. I know many members and people whom I count as close friends living in these countries.

One such person is Moscow State University Rector Victor A. Sadovnichy, and I once asked him what he thought of the BRICS countries. Saying that the economic emergence of these countries was to be expected, and that their future looked especially promising, Rector Sadovnichy explained:

> Our school has promoted exchanges with the leading BRICS universities over the years. We are partnering with institutions in China, India, and Brazil to carry out research addressing issues specific to each country, for example, and are expecting to achieve major advances through such initiatives.[9]

> The BRICS countries speak different languages and have adopted diverse religious and ideological traditions as the basis for their respective societies. Each has evolved from disparate historical and cultural milieus, creating what indeed may be described as a unique and autonomous civilisation unto itself. Thus, as these countries strengthen ties amongst themselves within the BRICS framework, it will serve as a worthy model of inter-civilisational dialogue and, in that sense, it is a phenomenon with profound implications.[10]

As for your observations on Indonesia and Nigeria, I have also come to believe in the immense potential of these two countries in the course of my many exchanges with their citizens. I am confident that these emerging nations will drive robust new progress for the entire world in the twenty-first century.

As with the BRICS countries, we see more and more nations

seeking transnational partnerships in various forms with other nations around the world. This trend entails a greater awareness in the belief that we are all co-inhabitants of this planet, regardless of our nationality or the region in which we live, which inevitably leads us to advance coexistence and mutual prosperity. My heartfelt hope is that SGI members, in 192 countries and territories worldwide, will continue contributing to mutual understanding and trust through dialogue and grassroots exchanges based on our Buddhist activities to promote peace, culture, and education.

A CENTURY OF CHALLENGES

IKEDA: Regrettably, while I want nothing more than to continue with your economics lessons, Professor Lau, I'm afraid we must bring our dialogue to an end. In closing, based on your many years of experience on this topic, what do you believe are some of the essential requirements for bright young scholars to build on and freely exercise their intellectual creativity, as you have?

LAU: I studied for many years in the United States. As I mentioned earlier, one key advantage of the US universities is the flexibility they allow undergraduate students to change their major subjects without losing significant time. The encouragement and promotion of inter- and multidisciplinary research is another major advantage of American educational and research institutions.

There is widespread openness in America to new ideas and to challenging questions posed to established scholarly authorities. It is only through the questioning of established authorities that breakthrough scientific progress can be made. Galileo challenged the accepted wisdom of his time; Einstein challenged Newton's Laws.

My experience is that when I teach a class in America, I am inundated with questions, but when I teach a class in East Asia—

China, Hong Kong, Japan, Korea, and Taiwan—I encounter very few questions. Respect for the teacher, for the elder, for authority, is an East Asian cultural trait, but that does inhibit questioning, which is always the indispensable first step to new scientific discovery.

IKEDA: In Japan, many universities are reforming their educational systems to produce creative, innovative thinkers.

Rector Sadovnichy expressed sentiments identical to yours. The rector, who is not only an acclaimed mathematician but also a full member of the Russian Academy of Science, raised one of his favorite topics in stating that science deals with a future fraught with the unknown, and that scientists should remain cognizant of this humbling truth. He stressed that they should always assume that the veracity of a preconceived notion is never absolute, and that science has continued to progress by upending extant fallacies.[11]

Thus, the answer to the question "What preconceived notions will be overturned by basic science in the twenty-first century?" contains the future of scientific study. He asserted that there are numerous opportunities for what is believed to be impossible today to become quite possible and real tomorrow.[12] I took it that the rector sees the reassessing and overturning of established worldviews as the grand task and challenge of young researchers the world over.

While this view of science is drawn from numerous examples recorded throughout human history, there are an equal number of instances in which discoveries of previously unknown truths in other disciplines have dramatically altered the way we see our world, spurring tectonic social changes. Rector Sadovnichy described this century as a "century of challenges," an era that will see a great transformation of human civilization across a broad range of realms, from science and economics to politics, education, and culture. I, too, have high hopes for the new discoveries of brilliant young minds that will make significant contributions to humanity.

To ensure the sound development of young people, Rector Sadovnichy strongly advocated that educators, drawing on values and insights embraced by religious traditions, should persevere in the effort to instill students with a robust moral foundation and foster their spirituality.[13] To empower youth, enabling them to rediscover and reaffirm the positive traditional values of their own cultures, to learn of and assimilate one another's spiritual cultures, ennobling these cultures further—this empowerment, I believe, is a crucial task that we are all obligated to bear.

As difficult as it is for me to say this, we must now conclude our dialogue. I am delighted at and grateful for the opportunity to conduct this candid, meaningful exchange of ideas and insights with you, Professor Lau.

The factors feeding instability are proliferating throughout the world. It is now more important than ever for Japan and China to engage each other in dialogue and facilitate exchange.

I offer my heartfelt appreciation for the time and energy you devoted to this discussion. And I look very much forward to sharing views with you again on another occasion in the months and years ahead.

APPENDIX 1

Proposal for the Normalization of Japan-China Relations
Daisaku Ikeda

Excerpts from Daisaku Ikeda's formal call for the normalization of bilateral ties between Japan and China at a meeting on September 8, 1968, attended by some 20,000 youth members enrolled as university students. Ikeda sought to reach out to China, given its isolation from the international community at the time.

It has been said for some time that when the conflict in Vietnam comes to an end, the focus of events will next shift to China. Some will no doubt say that in light of the present situations in Vietnam and Czechoslovakia, this is not the time to be discussing China. However, in terms of the position in which Japan finds itself, and from the perspective of "global transnationalism" put forward by the Soka Gakkai, the China question is one that is both fundamental and unavoidable. It is for this reason that I urge you to consider this issue with me today, as citizens of Japan aware of the realities of Japan's situation and as young people with hopes for a peaceful future.

It goes without saying that the issues involving China today constitute a stumbling block of major proportions on the path to realizing peace in the world. A glance at the history of the twenty years or so since the end of World War II reveals that Asia is the region in which most of the direct military confrontations between the two great blocs of East and West have taken place, resulting in the tragedy of war. One of these, as you are aware, was the Korean War, and the current war in Vietnam is another example.

On the side of the Western bloc, the country most directly involved is the United States, and on the side of the communist bloc is China, more so even than the Soviet Union. At present, China is excluded from the United Nations and has only the most tenuous diplomatic links with other nations. Seemingly hidden behind a "Bamboo Curtain," there is at best only a limited mutual understanding among China and other nations of one another's circumstances.

Therefore, without the provision of a venue where China, presently treated as a pariah within international society, can engage in discussions with other states on a fair, equal basis, there is little hope for the realization of peace in Asia and the world. This is something that troubles me deeply, and I am furthermore certain that resolving this situation, more than anything else, is the absolute condition for political stability and economic prosperity for Asian nations such as Korea, Taiwan, Vietnam, Thailand, and Laos.

What, then, are the concrete measures the international community should take to realize this? First, to officially recognize the People's Republic of China. Second, to prepare an appropriate seat for Beijing at the United Nations to encourage them to join the international arena. Third, to promote economic and cultural exchanges with China.

It should first be noted that Japan is uniquely positioned to make a decisive contribution to helping ease China's isolation, which is at present so tightly closed to the world. The factors in this are the proximity of China and Japan, both in terms of historical tradition and ethnic origins, as well as of course geography.

Despite this, Japan's present stance is one of seeking security under the nuclear umbrella of the United States, China's most hated adversary, while refusing to recognize China or to restore diplomatic ties. Exacerbating the situation, the small amount of trade Japan does conduct with China is being choked off year by year.

President Toda once wrote a poem that included the line "I vow to send the light of the sun to the people of Asia...." Our vision for Japan is based on the philosophy of the Middle Way, which is neither politically right nor left. As an Asian country, it is only natural that Japanese policy should place highest importance on enhancing the lives and welfare of the people of Asia. It is Japan's duty to do so.

The scars left by the war between China and Japan are still with us. But twenty-three years have passed since the end of the war, and most of you here today are of the generation that had no direct involvement in that conflict. Neither, for that matter, did today's youth in China. It is unacceptable that the young people on whom the future of both countries depends should be forced to bear the heavy burden of wounds from a past war.

When the younger generations in both China and Japan come to take a leading role in the affairs of their respective societies, the people of both countries will certainly join together in the cooperative work of constructing a brighter, happier world. It is only when all the peoples of Asia, with China and Japan playing pivotal roles, aid and support one another that the brutality of war and the dark clouds of poverty enveloping Asia will be dispelled, replaced by rays of hope and happiness.

I am by no means an unalloyed admirer of communism, and I believe myself to be fully conscious of the concern and caution that the good citizens of Japan feel as they try to anticipate what move China will make next. I simply believe that in terms of global trends, for the sake of peace in Asia and the rest of the world, it is essential that Japan be on friendly terms with all nations.

Further, in a nuclear age, it is no exaggeration to say that our success in saving humankind from annihilation hinges on our ability to develop friendships across national boundaries. This is at the heart of my reasons for discussing the problem of China with you here today.

Some may say my views are naïve, or that I haven't looked into the issues adequately. But until the issues concerning China are resolved, we cannot be said to have truly moved on from the post-War period.

The first matter I want to discuss is the normalization of relations between China and Japan. In 1952, Japan and the Nationalist government of Taiwan signed the Japan-ROC Treaty. The Japanese government has adopted the position that with this treaty, the issue of peace between China and Japan was resolved. This stance, however, represented an unrealistic view that in effect ignored the existence of the 710 million people living on the continent in mainland China.

The normalization of relations between the nations will only be meaningful when the people of both come to understand each other and interact in ways that are mutually beneficial, contributing by extension to world peace. Therefore, the 710 million people of mainland China are the real subject of our relations with China. To ignore this reality and instead be satisfied with having followed the letter of the law in establishing this treaty is unrealistic and unproductive, no matter how convinced one might be of the justice of one's stance.

In point of fact, [Premier] Zhou Enlai and other Chinese leaders have consistently expressed their view that the state of war between China and Japan has not yet been ended. So long as this perception persists, no matter how much Japan insists that the war is over, harmonious relations between the two countries can never become a reality. What I believe the Japanese government needs to do, therefore, is to engage in dialogue with the Beijing government, employing any means it can to realize such talks.

There are a number of issues that need to be resolved before full normalization of relations can take place. These include the question of compensation for the damage inflicted by Japan on China during World War II, as well foreign asset claims, mainly in Manchuria. These are complex issues, fraught with difficulty. And they cannot be solved without mutual understanding and deep trust between the two nations and most importantly, a shared aspiration for peace.

It is thus vital that Japan and China first forge real trust and mutual understanding, confirming their desire for peace. Starting from this conclusion, a so-called deductive process should be followed. It should be noted that the kind of inductive process which has been followed until now—employing small-scale diplomatic maneuvers and seeking to resolve marginal issues first, before ties between China and Japan are ultimately restored—has not worked.

Indeed, the quickest path to normalization lies in a meeting of the most senior-level leaders of the two countries, where they may confer and reconfirm their shared aspiration for peace. They will then be positioned to develop the fundamental direction for bilateral relations and the resolution of specific issues based on this broader perspective and understanding of each other. I have no doubt that if the leaders of China and Japan persist in efforts at constructive dialogue, no matter how difficult the issues may seem, it will be possible to find the means to their resolution.

Japan has developed under the constant influence of Chinese civilization since around the time of the earliest unification [of Japan] under one power or even before then. It is also from China that Buddhism was introduced into our country, along with sutras written in Chinese characters.

Our political philosophy and moral values directly reflect Confucianism. Many of the manners and customs that have completely become part of Japanese culture can be traced back to China.

From the perspective of ethnicity, a significant number of Chinese people were naturalized as Japanese during the Nara period (eighth century). The founder of the Tendai school of Buddhism in Japan, Saicho, is thought to have been of Chinese descent. The Uzumasa district of Kyoto, Japan's capital from 794, was then a community of clans of Chinese origin. In fact, there are numerous places throughout Japan whose names remind us of their Chinese origin.

It is only natural that two countries that share such long historic ties, ethnic proximity, and similarities in customs and traditions as China and Japan should have friendly relations. I must say therefore that it is extremely unnatural and irrational for Japan to keep its back turned upon China and just look on as our fellow Asians suffer, as is the case today.

A French critic has argued to the effect that Japan, which can be instrumental in leading the United States to change its policy in the Far East, should pursue an independent policy of promptly normalizing its relations with China to ease tensions in the international community. I totally agree with his view. I believe that the restoration of Sino-Japanese relations would not only benefit Japan but would also be a way for Japan to fulfill its proper role in the contemporary world.

I want to move on now to the issue of Chinese participation in the United Nations system. Generally known as the representation question, the issue is whether the regime in Beijing or that in Taiwan should occupy the Chinese seat at the United Nations. There are those who hold that, as a matter of common sense, this should be dealt with by creating new seats for both the mainland

People's Republic of China and for the Republic of China in Taiwan. Neither party, however, will agree to this. Each side insists that they are the [sole legitimate] representative of all the Chinese people.

In any event, public opinion is likely to gravitate toward supporting the Beijing government. The developed countries are gradually starting to recognize the People's Republic of China. Experts in international affairs predict that China's permanent representation at the United Nations will probably belong to Beijing within four or five years.[1]

Japan is an independent nation and as such naturally possesses the right to its own ideas and the pursuit of an independent foreign policy. Further, if we give due consideration to Japan's 2,000-year history of interactions with China, clearly recognize Japan's current position within international society, and focus on the ideal of peace in Asia and the world, it becomes clear that there is nothing to be gained from allowing the current state of affairs to continue indefinitely.

The times are changing even as we speak. Focusing on the future and taking action accordingly is the particular privilege of young people. And it is the responsibility of statesmen and leaders to enable and encourage them to do so.

In the autumn of 1968, the United Nations will hold its twenty-third General Assembly. This time, instead of lending its weight to the "important question" position of the United States, Japan should take active steps to advance Beijing's representation in the United Nations. There is no doubt that the present situation, in which a quarter of the world's population is effectively excluded from the United Nations, constitutes a serious impediment to the full functioning of the organization. It is my belief that resolving this issue would be a true demonstration of the central importance of the United Nations and a great contribution to world peace.

Next, let me offer some thoughts on the issue of Sino-Japanese trade. Let us compare China's trade volume with socialist countries against that with capitalist countries. There was heavy dependence on the Soviet Union in the 1950s, with trade with the communist bloc being responsible for some 70 percent of China's total trade. In the 1960s, however, trade with capitalist countries has accounted for approximately 70 percent.

French journalist Robert Guillain pointed out (in *Dans trente ans, la Chine*, 1965) that trade with China was probably more beneficial to Japan than to any other country. I think it would be most valuable and prudent for Japan to build close relations with China, with its rich resources and huge market, in light of our geographic proximity and long-term development. I want to stress that such ties would not only bring about economic benefits but also directly contribute to the prosperity of Asia and global peace.

As mentioned earlier, Asia is the region of greatest instability in the world. As such it contains the gravest threats to world peace. Clearly, the fundamental causes of this instability are poverty and the gulf of mistrust and confrontation between capitalist and communist Asia. If poverty in Asia is to be fundamentally relieved, Japan must renew its approach—one that has until now involved turning its back on half of Asia—and instead work for the prosperity of all of Asia.

I must emphasize that a successful Japanese initiative to establish friendly relationships with China has the potential to defuse—eventually in a decisive manner—East-West tensions and confrontation in Asia.

The present situation is undeniably fraught with uncertainty. If we concern ourselves only with immediate, short-term interests, pursuing rapid economic growth for Japan alone, then our current foreign policy stance would probably appear to be the safest option. But if the conditions I have discussed are allowed to continue as they are, the danger of war will only increase, easily threatening Japan's current economic prosperity. This possibility is of great concern to me.

With the second-largest GNP in the free world, Japan is now enjoying a period of unprecedented prosperity. But this prosperity is nothing more than a house of cards, resting on the backs of the great mass of its underpaid citizens and on the poverty of the peoples of Asia. One French economist dubbed Japan's prosperity "prosperity without a soul," and another sociologist went so far as to judge the Japanese a "well-off, but emasculated nation."

Whether as a state or as a people, in international society today, engaging purely in the pursuit of one's own profit is no longer acceptable. It is surely by adopting a broad global perspective and by seeking to contribute to peace, prosperity, and the advancement of culture that we will prove our worth as a people in the coming century. I cannot emphasize this point enough. Now is the time for Japan to adopt a global perspective and, for the sake of prosperity in Asia and peace in the world, put maximum effort into the most important means of achieving these goals: normalization of relations with China, the realization of Chinese representation at the United Nations, and the promotion of trade with China.

There will of course be those who dispute my view of China in various ways. In this regard, I leave it to the judgment of you wise young people. I took it upon myself today to put forward my beliefs on a problem that Japan and all of you young people here will have to deal with for the sake of the world's future. It would give me great satisfaction if you were to give some consideration to what you have heard today.

Any position of the type I have discussed today—advocating friendship between China and Japan—will inevitably be misinterpreted as leftist. This is an entirely superficial way of thinking. It is only natural for us as Buddhists, out of a commitment to humanity and the ideal of global transnationalism, to desire peace and stability for Japan and the world.

Anyone who makes the effort to understand the true nature of this perspective will quickly realize that it is not constrained by the political categories of left and right. Making hasty judgments based on the superficial appearance about whether something is left or right is a serious error. Ultimately, the most important thing about a way of thinking is the worldview in which it is rooted. Any discussion that ignores this is meaningless. For us, the underlying idea is the Buddhist philosophy of the unity of the physical and spiritual, the material and mental, aspects of life. Our approach, that of the Middle Way, is firmly grounded in this.

Bonds of Bilateral Friendship Must Never Be Broken
Daisaku Ikeda

Excerpts from the 2013 peace proposal "Compassion, Wisdom and Courage: Building a Global Society of Peace and Creative Coexistence"

I would like to share, from both a short- and a long-term perspective, some thoughts on ways to improve the currently strained relations between China and Japan. I am motivated by my conviction that this is indispensable to building a global society of peace and coexistence.

Last year marked the significant juncture of the fortieth anniversary of the restoration of Sino-Japanese diplomatic ties. However, a number of events and exchange programs celebrating the anniversary were canceled or postponed due to escalating tensions and frictions. Relations between the two countries have deteriorated to a post-World War II low, and economic relations have also chilled significantly.

I, however, am not at all pessimistic about the future of Sino-Japanese relations. In the words of the traditional Chinese maxim, "drops of water can pierce even a rock." In just this way, friendship between Japan and China has been nurtured in the postwar period by the devoted efforts of pioneers who, even before the normalization of diplomatic relations, worked tenaciously to break through the obstacles that stood between the two countries. These bonds of friendship have been steadily cultivated and strengthened through countless exchanges over the years, and they will not be easily broken.

When I called for the normalization of Sino-Japanese diplomatic relations in September 1968, it was almost unthinkable in Japan to even mention the possibility of friendship with China. In that sense, the situation was even more severe than it is today. But it was my belief that Japan had no future without friendly relations with its neighbors, and that stable and harmonious ties with China were essential for Asia and the world to advance along the great path to peace.

In 1972, diplomatic relations were finally normalized. Six years after I made that initial call, in December 1974, I was able to visit Beijing and meet with Chinese Premier Zhou Enlai and Vice Premier Deng Xiaoping. Through these discussions, I learned that they viewed both the Japanese and the Chinese people as victims of the Japanese militarist regime. This further deepened my determination to develop an indestructible friendship between our two peoples in order to prevent war between us from ever happening again.

Ever since, I have been passionately devoted to promoting friendship exchanges, with a special focus on members of the younger generation. In 1975, I served as personal guarantor when Soka University welcomed the first six government-financed exchange students from the People's Republic of China to study in Japan. Now, nearly forty years later, 100,000 Chinese students are studying here, and 15,000 Japanese students are pursuing their studies in China.

Over the years, China and Japan have created a history of

exchanges in cultural, educational, and many other fields, including, for example, a total of 349 sister-city arrangements. We have also developed a tradition of mutual support in times of hardship such as the 2008 earthquake in Sichuan and the 2011 earthquake in northeastern Japan. Despite occasional periods of tension, the currents of friendship between the two countries have grown steadily stronger over the years.

This current is the accumulation of friendships developed through innumerable face-to-face interactions and exchanges, each of which makes its own small yet invaluable contribution. For this reason, it will not easily run dry no matter what trial or obstacle it encounters. And we must ensure that never happens.

In a lecture I delivered at Peking University in May 1990, I urged, "No matter what issues might come between us, the bonds of friendship must never be broken."[1] Now more than ever we need to reaffirm that conviction.

The political and economic arenas are always impacted by the ebb and flow of the times. Indeed, times of tranquility are perhaps the exception rather than the rule. This is why, when faced with a crisis, it is important to adamantly uphold the two central pledges in the Treaty of Peace and Friendship between Japan and the People's Republic of China (1978): To refrain from the use or threat of force, and not to seek regional hegemony.

So long as we uphold these principles, we will without fail find ways to overcome the present crisis. Even more than when things are going well, it is times of adversity that present opportunities to deepen understanding and strengthen ties. I strongly encourage Japan and China to reconfirm their commitment to uphold the two pledges of the Treaty of Peace and Friendship and promptly set up a high-level forum for dialogue aimed at preventing any further deterioration of relations.

The first order of business for such a forum should be to institute a moratorium on all actions that could be construed as provocative. This should be followed by a scrupulous analysis of the steps by which the confrontation evolved—how actions were perceived and what reactions were provoked. This would facilitate the development of guidelines for more effective responses to future crises. Doubtless, some sharp differences of opinion would be expressed, but unless we are prepared to face each other on those terms, hopes for the restoration of friendly relations between the two countries—for greater stability in Asia and for a peaceful world—will continue to elude us.

Immediately after the end of the Cold War, I met for the first time with then Soviet President Mikhail Gorbachev, in July 1990. I opened our conversation by saying: "I have come to have an argument with you. Let's make sparks fly, and talk about everything honestly and openly, for the sake of humanity and for the sake of Japan-Soviet relations!" I expressed myself in this way to convey my hopes of having a real and frank discussion instead of a merely formal meeting, at a time when the prospects for Japan-Soviet relations were uncertain.

The more difficult the situation appears to be, the more important it is to engage in dialogue based on a commitment to peace and creative coexistence. Heated and earnest dialogue can reveal the emotions—the fears, concerns and aspirations—that underlie the positions and assertions of each side.

In this context, I propose that China and Japan institute the practice of holding regular summit meetings.

This month marks the fiftieth anniversary of the signing of the Élysée Treaty by France and Germany. The treaty helped the two countries overcome their history of war and bloodshed, with relations becoming significantly closer due to the provisions for regular meetings of Heads of State and Government at least twice a year and for ministerial-level meetings at least once every three months in the fields of foreign affairs, defense, and education. I believe that the current crisis between Japan and China presents a unique opportunity to establish a similar framework, creating an environment that enables their leaders to conduct face-to-face dialogue under any circumstances.

Further, I suggest that Japan and China together launch an organization for environmental cooperation in East Asia. This could be an interim goal to be achieved by 2015 and would lay the foundations of a new partnership focused on peace and creative coexistence and joint action for the sake of humanity.

Amelioration of environmental conditions would benefit both countries. This new organization would create opportunities for young people from China and Japan to work together toward a common goal. It would also establish a pattern of contributing together to the peace and stability of East Asia and the creation of a sustainable global society.

When I called for the normalization of diplomatic relations back in September 1968, I urged the young people of both countries to come together in friendship to build a better world. The foundation for this, I believe, has now been laid in a quiet, uncelebrated way through the exchanges and interactions that have been conducted to date.

Now, I believe, the focus should turn to something more visible and durable. The time has come to take a medium- to long-term perspective and develop more concrete models of cooperation across a range of new fields. I am convinced that it is through such sustained and determined efforts that the bonds of friendship between China and Japan will develop into something indestructible, something that will be passed down with pride from generation to generation.

APPENDIX 3

Regional Cooperation for Resilience
Daisaku Ikeda

Excerpts from the 2014 peace proposal "Value Creation for Global Change: Building Resilient and Sustainable Societies"

[A] key area I would like to discuss relates to international cooperation to minimize the damage caused by extreme weather and other disasters.

According to a report of the World Meteorological Organization issued last July, more than 370,000 people died as a result of extreme weather and climate events during the first decade of the twenty-first century, including Hurricane Katrina, floods in Pakistan, and drought in the Amazon Basin.[1] Extreme weather events have continued with unabated frequency into the current decade. In 2013 alone, Typhoon Haiyan caused severe damage in the Philippines and Vietnam, heavy rain brought flooding in central Europe and India, and much of the Northern Hemisphere experienced record high temperatures as a result of heat waves. In addition to the direct damage, climate change seriously impacts sectors vital to the livelihood of countless people around the world, including agriculture, fisheries and forestry. The world-wide financial impact of weather-related damage is estimated at US$200 billion a year.[2]

The Conference of the Parties to the United Nations Framework Convention on Climate Change has begun to address the loss and damage associated with climate change as a separate issue from the reduction of greenhouse gas emissions. The nineteenth session that took place in Warsaw, Poland, last November agreed upon the Warsaw International Mechanism for Loss and Damage. Under this mechanism, developed countries will be asked to provide financial assistance to developing countries impacted by climate change. The mechanism lacks legally binding force, however, and the next opportunity for review will not be until 2016, so there are questions about its actual effectiveness.

Last November, the United Nations University Institute for Environment and Human Security issued a report, warning: "Current levels of adaptation and mitigation efforts are insufficient to avoid negative impacts from climate stressors."[3] Clearly, a new and more effective approach is an urgent priority.

Here, I would like to propose the establishment of regional cooperative mechanisms to reduce damage from extreme weather and disasters, strengthening resilience in regions such as Asia and Africa. These would function alongside global measures developed under the UNFCCC.

There are three aspects to the response to extreme weather events and other disasters: disaster preparedness, disaster relief, and post-disaster recovery. It is not uncommon for relief assistance to be provided by other countries, but international cooperation in the other two areas still tends to be the exception. Even when there has been abundant emergency relief assistance in the immediate aftermath of a disaster, it remains extremely difficult for a country to recover post-disaster and strengthen preparedness relying only on its own resources. Establishing a mechanism for mutual assistance based on lessons learned from shared experiences is therefore an urgent priority.

At present, the UN engages in conflict prevention, conflict resolution, and post-conflict peacebuilding and recovery as an integrated process under the auspices of the Peacebuilding Commission. In the same way, disaster preparedness, disaster relief, and post-disaster recovery need to be treated as an integrated process. To this end, I would like to suggest that neighboring countries set up a system of cooperation for responding to extreme weather and other disasters. Such systems should be built on relations among neighboring countries because, unlike relief efforts immediately following a disaster, preparedness and recovery require sustained cooperation. Such cooperation is facilitated by geographic proximity, as is the sharing of lessons and knowledge on preparedness among countries exposed to similar threats.

This alone would be significant, but it could bring immeasurable value to an entire region once cooperation regarding extreme weather and disasters among neighboring countries begins to fully function—the possibility of transforming countries' understanding of and approach to security.

A report released at the International Conference on Climate Security in the Asia-Pacific Region held in Seoul, Korea, in March 2013, found that at least 110 countries around the world consider the effects of climate change to represent a "serious national security issue."[4] This constitutes an important change as, in the past, many governments viewed climate change as just another environmental issue and accorded it a low priority. This has changed in recent years, and more and more governments now see the need to treat it as a threat to national security.

Noteworthy here is the fact that measures to enhance security in line with this new perception will not lead to what has been called the "security dilemma," a vicious cycle in which the steps a state takes to heighten security are perceived by other states as an increased threat, causing them to respond with similar measures, only leading to further mistrust and tension.

Above all, the unpredictable nature of extreme weather and natural disasters and the sense of vulnerability they provoke open the door to empathy and solidarity across national borders. Numerous countries have demonstrated this in their willingness to help those in need, rushing relief teams and offering assistance to the affected country in the immediate aftermath of a disaster.

This is a point I discussed in the dialogue I am conducting with the renowned peace scholar Professor Kevin P. Clements. Both our countries were hit by earthquakes around the same time in 2011—New Zealand by the Christchurch Earthquake and Japan by the Tohoku Earthquake. Professor Clements described the wide-scale international cooperation he witnessed on that occasion, and noted:

> It underlines the ways in which we all know in our heart of hearts that there is a common humanity that unites all of us irrespective of our cultural, linguistic, or national differences. It's a pity that this common humanity is often only realized in times of crisis. It is important, therefore, that we maintain this "disaster spirit" in normal times as well.[5]

Indeed, as neighboring countries make sustained efforts to cooperate in strengthening resilience and recovery assistance, the spirit of mutual help and support can become the shared culture of the region.

The knowledge, technology, and know-how that facilitates cooperation in these areas is such that its value to all parties is enhanced through sharing. This is in contrast to the secrecy that typically surrounds military-based technologies and information.

The more that countries share information and technology in resilience-related fields, the greater the opportunity to minimize damage, which in turn reduces disaster risk and enhances security throughout the region.

This is in line with the concept of "knowledge as a global public good,"[6] described by the economist Joseph E. Stiglitz employing the following words of Thomas Jefferson, the third president of the United States: "He who receives an idea from me, receives instruction himself without lessening mine; as he who lights his taper at mine, receives light without darkening me."[7]

Disaster resilience consists of four elements: robustness (the strength of systems to withstand stress without loss of function); redundancy (systems that allow for substitution); resourcefulness (the capacity to mobilize society's physical and intellectual resources); and rapidity (the capacity to identify priorities to prevent further disruption and speed up the process of recovery). We can receive ideas about these elements from others without in any way lessening their capacity, as Jefferson's analogy makes clear.

I urge that the pioneering initiative for such regional cooperation be taken in Asia, a region that has been severely impacted by disasters. A successful model here will inspire collaborative work to strengthen resilience and recovery assistance in other regions.

A foundation for this already exists: the ASEAN Regional Forum, whose members include the ASEAN countries as well as China, Japan, North Korea, and South Korea. Making disaster relief one of its security priorities, ARF has in place a framework for regularly discussing better ways of cooperation. ARF has conducted three disaster relief exercises to date, consisting of civil-military coordinated drills involving medical, sanitation, and water supply teams from various countries.

In his 1903 book *Jinsei chirigaku* (A Geography of Human Life), Tsunesaburo Makiguchi called for a transformation from zero-sum military competition to "humanitarian competition." The exercises conducted by ARF may foreshadow this kind of transition.

In an era dominated by imperialism and colonialism, Makiguchi observed a transition in the arenas of competition among states from the military to the political to the economic. He called for a departure from these modes of competition, which seek to secure one's own prosperity at the expense of others, advocating instead that states direct their efforts to achieving the objectives of humanitarian competition.

Makiguchi explored the possibility of a qualitative transformation of military, political, and economic competition, a shift to "engaging consciously in collective life" by choosing to "do things for the sake of others, because by benefiting others, we benefit ourselves." Makiguchi described his humanitarian perspective as follows: "What is important is to set aside egotistical motives, striving to protect and improve not only one's own life, but also the lives of others."[8]

More than a century after he made this call, ARF's disaster relief exercises can be seen as an opportunity for states to pursue a qualitative transformation in the nature of military competition.

As countries continue to work together to strengthen cooperation for disaster relief, resolving mistrust and ill feelings toward one another in the process, they can develop collaborative relationships robust enough to be extended to post-disaster recovery operations. As a means to promote this, I would like to propose an Asia recovery resilience agreement, as a framework drawing on the experience of the ARF.

One important avenue for promoting disaster preparedness, an integral aspect of resilience, is face-to-face exchanges and cooperation among local government bodies in various countries through sister-city agreements. I urge that Japan, China, and South Korea take the initiative in mutually strengthening resilience through such sister-city relationships.

Currently, there are 354 sister-city agreements between Japan and China, 151 between Japan and South Korea, and 149 between China and South Korea. Further, the Japan-China-South Korea Trilateral Local Government Conference has taken place annually since 1999 to further promote this kind of interaction.

Building upon this foundation, ties of friendship and trust could be made even stronger through collaborative efforts to strengthen resilience, including disaster prevention and mitigation. Members of the younger generation should take the lead in this. Sister-city exchanges and cooperation would then evolve into collective action connecting cities across national borders, eventually creating spaces of peaceful coexistence throughout the region.

If we are incapable of making sincere efforts to cultivate friendly relations with our neighbors, how can we presume to speak of contributing to global peace? The spirit of mutual aid demonstrated in times of disaster should be the basis of day-to-day relations among neighboring countries.

I strongly urge that a Japan-China-South Korea summit be held at the earliest opportunity to initiate dialogue toward this kind of cooperation. Ideally, this should include cooperation on environmental problems along the lines I proposed last year. The third World Conference on Disaster Risk Reduction to be held in Sendai, Japan, in March 2015, should serve as an impetus for further talks to explore the modalities of concretizing such cooperation.

By taking up this challenge, we have the opportunity to generate new waves of value creation—not only in Asia, but throughout the world.

Sharing in Best Practices for Human Talent Development
Daisaku Ikeda

Excerpts from the 2015 peace proposal "A Shared Pledge for a More Humane Future: To Eliminate Misery from the Earth"

The last field for shared action I would like to address is the construction of a sustainable global society.

In order to respond to environmental challenges such as climate change, we must share experiences and lessons learned as we work to prevent a worsening of conditions and effect the transition toward a zero-waste society. Such efforts will be crucial in the achievement of the SDGs [Sustainable Development Goals], and I would like to stress the indispensable role of cooperation among neighboring countries to this end.

Concretely, I call on China, South Korea, and Japan to join together to create a regional model that will embody best practices that can be shared with the world, including those relating to the development of human talent. In November last year, the first China-Japan summit meeting in two and a half years was held. As someone who has long sought and worked for friendship between the two countries, I was deeply gratified to see this first step toward the improvement of bilateral relations following a sustained chill.

In the wake of the summit, in December, the Japan-China Energy Conservation Forum was restarted, and on January 12 this year, consultations were held regarding the Japan-China Maritime Communication Mechanism. This mechanism can play a crucial role in preventing the escalation of any incident, and I hope that efforts to begin operation within the year as agreed to by the two leaders will proceed smoothly.

This year marks the fiftieth anniversary of the normalization of relations between South Korea and Japan. While there is still a need to defuse political tensions between the two countries, we should not lose sight of the fact that people-to-people interactions have continued to expand, with some five million people now traveling between Korea and Japan annually, a number even greater than that for China and Japan. When bilateral relations were normalized in 1965, the annual figure was a mere 10,000 people. Although public opinion surveys reveal that large percentages of people in both Korea and Japan do not have a favorable opinion of the other country, more than 60 percent acknowledge the importance of the relationship.

In addition to such interactions, I have high expectations regarding the forms of trilateral cooperation that have been steadily developing for the past dozen or so years. Since the start in 1999 of trilateral cooperation in the environmental field, there are today more than fifty consultative mechanisms including eighteen ministerial meetings and more than one hundred cooperative projects. To encourage the further development of such cooperation, it is important that trilateral China-Korea-Japan summits be renewed following the three-year hiatus brought about by heightened political tensions.

As the adoption of the SDGs nears, such summits should be restarted at the earliest possible date to solidify the trend in improved relations, while building toward a formal agreement to make the region a model of sustainability. The leaders of the three countries should mark the seventieth anniversary of the end of World War II by embodying the lessons of that conflict in a pledge never to go to war again and should initiate efforts to build robust mutual trust through regional cooperation in support of the new challenge of the SDGs being undertaken by the UN.

In my meetings with political, intellectual, and cultural leaders from China and Korea including Chinese Premier Zhou Enlai and Korean Prime Minister Lee Soo-sung, we have discussed the way that Japan and China and Japan and Korea can deepen bonds of friendship in order to make lasting contributions to the world.

Jean Monnet, who played a key role in helping France and Germany overcome their centuries-long animosity, asserted during negotiations among European countries in 1950: "We are here to undertake a common task—not to negotiate for our own national advantage, but to seek it to the advantage of all.[1]

In September 2011, a Trilateral Cooperation Secretariat was established by China, Korea, and Japan. One role for this secretariat is identifying potential cooperative projects. I hope that the three countries will work together for the advantage of all in every one of the fields set out in the new SDGs.

As mentioned earlier, the SGI will be cosponsoring a side event at the Third UN World Conference on Disaster Risk Reduction in which civil society representatives of the three countries will meet to discuss regional cooperation toward disaster prevention and post-disaster recovery. This is being held with the support of the Trilateral Cooperation Secretariat, and I am confident it represents the kind of positive engagement at the grassroots level that will complement intergovernmental regional cooperation toward the realization of the SDGs.

In this regard, I would like to make two proposals for expanding grassroots exchanges.

The first of these has a focus on youth. A key turning point in postwar relations between France and Germany was the 1963 Élysée Treaty, which initiated an era of greatly expanded exchanges among youth. "Centuries-old enmity can give way to profound friendship."[2] This phrase comes from an article jointly written by French Foreign Minister Laurent Fabius and German Foreign Minister Guido Westerwelle in 2013, marking the fiftieth anniversary of the Élysée Treaty. And indeed, the more than eight million young people who have had the opportunity to live or study in the partner country have played a critical role in generating firm bonds connecting the two societies.

Eight years ago, a program of youth exchanges was initiated between China, Korea, and Japan, and I hope this year (2014) will be the occasion for greatly expanding the scale of this program. In addition to increasing cultural or educational exchanges such as those among high school or college students, I would like to see the establishment of a China-Korea-Japan youth partnership through which young people can actively collaborate on efforts to realize the SDGs or other trilateral cooperation initiatives.

For individual participants, the experience of working together on the daunting challenges of environmental or disaster-related issues is an invaluable one, impressing in their young lives the confidence that they are creating their own future. Further, such treasures of a lifetime will without doubt become the foundation of friendship and trust that will extend far into the future.

In the three decades since the signing of an exchange agreement between the Soka Gakkai youth division and the All-China Youth Federation in 1985, there have been regular exchanges. In May 2014, a new ten-year exchange agreement was signed, with the promise to continue to work together to enhance friendship between the two countries. For their part, the Soka Gakkai youth members in Kyushu have engaged in a wide range of exchange activities with Korea. All these activities arise from the belief that networks among young people fostered through face-to-face encounter and exchange are ultimately the most critical factor in building a more peaceful and humane world in the twenty-first century.

My second proposal is to greatly increase the number of sister-city exchanges between the three countries, aiming toward 2030, the SDG target date.

When I met with Premier Zhou Enlai forty years ago, our most salient shared interest was in deepening friendly relations between citizens of the two countries. In my September 1968 call for the normalization of Sino-Japanese relations, I stated: "The normalization of relations between nations will only be meaningful when the people of both come to understand each other and interact in ways that are mutually beneficial, contributing by extension to world peace." In like manner, Premier Zhou held that lasting Sino-Japanese friendship could only be realized when the people of both countries truly understood and trusted each other. When we met, he spoke of his own youthful experience of living and studying in Japan for a year and a half, and I cannot help but feel that this shaped his perspective.

In 1916, the year before Zhou came to Japan to study, the Japanese political philosopher Sakuzo Yoshino wrote the following against a backdrop of worsening Sino-Japanese relations: "If there is trust and respect between the citizens, even if hostility or misunderstanding regarding political or economic issues arise, these will be like waves stirred on the surface of the ocean by the wind, but which leave the deeply flowing currents of friendly relations undisturbed."[3]

This expresses my own long-standing conviction. If people of different nationalities can engage in exchanges of the heart, sharing concern for each other's happiness, the great tree of friendship that is fostered will withstand all wind and snows, extending branches of lush growth far into the future.

Currently there are 356 local government sister-city agreements between China and Japan, 156 between Japan and South Korea, and 151 between China and South Korea. We should continue to extend such sister-city exchanges while fostering the crucial one-to-one bonds of friendship.

APPENDIX 5

Lessons from the Global Financial Crisis
Lawrence J. Lau

The author's research paper on the global financial crisis, published in 2011

What caused the global financial crisis of 2007–2009? The principal causes were: (1) Easy money in the United States; (2) failures of regulation and supervision; and (3) defects in the institutional design of the financial sector.

One of the principal causes of the global financial crisis is regulatory and supervisory failure in the United States and Europe. Why were the serious regulatory failures that allowed the global financial crisis to occur possible?

The first fundamental reason is the overly strong faith on the part of the US financial regulators that whatever could go wrong "the market would take care of it." It turned out that the market, in the absence of proper regulatory oversight, could not take care of it by itself, at least not in time to avert a full-blown crisis.

The second fundamental reason is a phenomenon known as

regulatory capture—over time, the regulatory agencies have been "captured" by those firms they are supposed to regulate, through lobbying and other efforts by the latter, and are thus frequently persuaded to relax regulatory requirements in favor of these firms.

Regulatory failures have been manifested in many areas. The principal areas of regulatory failures are:

(1) Unwillingness and inability to restrain irrational exuberance;
(2) Excessive leverage of financial institutions (as well as some non-financial firms) and of the financial sector as a whole;
(3) Failure to ensure competitive markets; and
(4) Failure to control moral hazard.

Irrational exuberance is not uncommon—economic and financial bubbles have occurred from time to time all over the World for centuries, driven by (initially) self-fulfilling asset price expectations and abetted by the heavy use of leverage.

However, bubbles can and should be contained and restrained by the suitable and timely restrictions on the use of leverage. For examples, the maximum loan-to-value ratio of home mortgages can be lowered; and the margin requirements for the purchase of common stocks can be raised. Other instruments include increasing the stamp duty/transaction taxes, and increasing the capital gains tax rate on assets (property and securities), especially on assets held only for a short duration. There are many other different ways of lowering the expected net after-tax return of speculative investments and thus discouraging them.

Impact of Excessive Leverage

Excessive leverage, that is, an excessively high debt to equity ratio, of a firm implies that it is more likely to fail, other things being equal, because an ever so slight temporary setback can turn the net worth of the firm negative and hence push the firm into bankruptcy. Moreover, excessive leverage encourages moral hazard (recklessness) on the part of the borrowing firm because the managers/owners/shareholders lose relatively little when the firm fails, with the bulk of the losses borne by the creditors, but retain the bulk of the profits when the firm succeeds. Excessive leverage of a firm also magnifies the negative spillover effects of bankruptcy of the borrowing firm—not only does it have to shut down but its failure also impacts negatively all of its creditors, contractors, lenders, and suppliers, firms that may otherwise be well managed but happens to do business with it. Excessive leverage also in turn increases the risk of other firms having such a firm as a "counter-party" in "hedging" transactions.

Furthermore, excessive leverage, if widespread, enables and magnifies the domino effect of insolvency and bankruptcy of a firm on the entire financial system by causing the failures of its creditors, contractors, lenders, and suppliers. Their failures may in turn trigger additional failures if they are also excessively leveraged themselves. Excessive leverage also enables speculators (e.g. hedge funds) to take sufficiently dominant long or short positions in markets of certain financial instruments (for example, credit default swaps [CDSs]) to affect the market outcomes and to engage in predatory speculation on a large scale.

Because of the potentially large negative externalities that excessively leveraged financial institutions can create, they should be prevented from becoming so. The US regulators (Securities and Exchange Commission) made the mistake of relaxing the capital requirement on the US securities firms some time in the early 2000s, which in turn allowed these firms to achieve their high leverage, at the request of a group of large US securities firms. In addition, many financial institutions undertook off-balance-sheet activities (for examples, "special-purpose vehicles (SPVs)," "special investment vehicles (SIVs)," "structured investment vehicles (also known as SIVs)," "shadow banking," and the like) to hide their true "excessive leverage."

In financial crisis after financial crisis, it has always been the excessive leverage that causes the domino effect on the rest of the economy. When a badly managed but highly leveraged firm collapses, it brings down with it all of its creditors, contractors, lenders, suppliers, and counter-parties in its financial derivative transactions, in addition to its own shareholders. The excessive leverage of Western banks did not just happen overnight. It was the combined result of lax regulation and supervision, "regulatory capture," and the competitive pressure in the financial markets. Banks compete with one another. If a bank is allowed to have a higher leverage, its return on equity will be higher than its competitors, at least in the short run. In order to compete effectively, its competitor banks will need to emulate the high leverage, resulting in excessive leverage across the board.

FAIR MARKET PRINCIPLE AND INFORMATION DISCLOSURE

Financial markets can be efficient only if there is no information asymmetry, that is, only when all market participants have access to substantially the same information. When not all market participants have the same information, the market system is no longer efficient or fair (the playing field is not level). In addition, the markets can be efficient only if investors with large positions do not abuse their monopolistic or monopsonistic powers. When one market player has a large enough market share to influence the market outcome, but fails to disclose it, the market outcome is neither efficient nor fair. Large investors should be required to disclose their positions and also when they trade. In most public stock exchanges, disclosure of significant ownership interest is required of a single investor or a group of investors acting in concert (e.g., over 5 percent ownership of a publicly listed company). However, this requirement has yet to be extended to markets for commodities, currencies, forward and futures contracts, options, and other traded financial derivatives. Regulatory agencies have a responsibility of assuring symmetry of information and full disclosure in order to ensure the competitiveness and fairness of the public markets.

Because of the lack of full disclosure of information and the opaqueness of non-public markets, players with large dominant positions can make use of their market power to manipulate the markets without revealing any of their transactions. Under these circumstances, the interests of small investors are not adequately protected. There should also be some rules as to the maximum share of a given financial instrument that an investor is permitted to hold at any given time in certain markets, like the rule that no firm is permitted to bid for more than 25 percent of a given US Treasury issue, for example, in the oil futures market, for delivery or settlement as of a certain date.

The regulatory agencies failed to demand that large investors disclose major positions on securities and other traded financial instruments, such as commodity futures, options, other financial derivatives, and structured products held by them, as is required for shares and contracts traded on public exchanges, resulting in severe information asymmetry which in turn affects the efficiency and fairness of the markets and the proper governance of firms. The regulatory agencies also failed to demand full and complete disclosure of financial information and large financial transactions, especially transactions conducted off public exchanges, by large financial institutions and other publicly listed companies. For example, when the same financial derivative instrument is sold to different market participants at different prices at the same time (which can happen since the transactions are not executed on a public exchange), the market will fail to be efficient.

Information asymmetry is also created when the financial balance sheets of a corporation fail to provide a true picture of the corporation's conditions, for example, when the corporation has significant off-balance-sheet activities. Off-balance-sheet activities conducted by Enron Corporation were the principal cause of its collapse. Enron ultimately had to recognize on its balance sheets all the losses incurred in its off-balance-sheet activities. The venerable auditing firm Arthur Andersen was also dragged down along with Enron. It was the largest corporate bankruptcy in the United States before the failure of Lehman Brothers in 2008. By allowing off-balance-sheet activities, corporations are implicitly encouraged to take "hidden actions," and that further increases moral hazard. Such hidden actions enable the firm to take on excessive leverage and circumvent regulations on capital adequacy without the knowledge of its board of directors, its shareholders, the public and even the regulatory agencies.

However, neither the US Securities and Exchange Commission nor the US Congress learned the lessons of the failure of Enron Corporation and have continued to allow publicly listed companies to engage in off-balance-sheet activities. The Sarbanes-Oxley Act of the United States, which is supposed to prevent a recurrence of failures such as Enron, fails to address this most important issue at all, despite its many costly and intrusive provisions on corporate governance and auditing. Many of the world's largest banks, Citicorp, HSBC, UBS, etc., suffered huge losses in this financial crisis because of their off-balance-sheet activities in the form of "special investment vehicles (SIVs)" or "structured investment vehicles (also known as SIVs)," and ultimately had to take these off-balance-sheet activities onto their balance sheets and write off hundreds of billions (US$) of bad assets. This is one of the principal reasons for the high actual as opposed to disclosed leverage of many financial institutions in the 2007–2009 crisis. Even sovereign governments such as Greece engaged in off-balance-sheet activities with the help of some financial institutions. Had off-balance-sheet activities been outlawed, Greece might still be in trouble, but the problems would have come to the surface earlier and it would not have been in such bad a shape.

If publicly listed companies had been forbidden to engage in off-balance-sheet activities, all of these losses could have been avoided, and the securitized sub-prime mortgage loans would not have found such a ready group of purchasers. Moreover, a great deal of the shadow banking activities, e.g., those involving the so-called auction-rate securities, had the implicit and explicit support of the major banks but were not regulated nor reflected as potential or contingent liabilities of the banks.

UBIQUITOUS MORAL HAZARD

It is also well known that moral hazard, if not appropriately recognized, discouraged, and restrained, can play havoc with the markets and institutions and increase the overall risk to the financial sector and the entire economy. The regulators should develop rules and regulations and promote practices that discourage moral hazard on the part of the different market participants in the financial sector. However, the regulators failed to do so—there was moral hazard everywhere, ranging from the originating mortgage lenders, credit rating agencies, purchasers of credit default swaps, asymmetric incentive compensation of executives of firms, especially financial institutions and hedge funds, and being "too big to fail," to name only a few. Each of these moral hazards will be discussed in turn.

SUB-PRIME LOAN CRISIS

The sub-prime mortgage loan crisis in the United States, which was the beginning phase of the 2007–2009 global financial crisis, was possible in large part because of the failure of the regulators to control the moral hazard of the originating mortgage lenders. The originating lenders of sub-prime mortgage loans made residential mortgage loans to borrowers with no apparent capacity for or means of repayment of either interest or principal, based only on a vague hope of appreciation of the prices of the properties in the future. The originating lenders were allowed to sell these mortgage loans off through securitization with no residual liability. Thus, they had no incentive to make sure that the loans would perform—that the borrowers were credit-worthy and had the means of repayment and that the collaterals were worth their value. There was little attempt to check the credit-worthiness of the borrowers or the real value of the properties, since the mortgage loans would be sold to other investors without recourse to the originating lenders. The volume of substandard mortgage loans (including both Alt-A and sub-prime loans) began growing rapidly in 2000 and by 2006 accounted for almost half of all mortgage loans made in the United States. It was these sub-prime mortgage loans that drove up the home prices successively in all segments of the market. If the originating mortgage lending institutions were required to retain some form of residual liability, e.g., a mandatory buy-back if the loan does not perform during the first three years of the life of the loan, or a holdback of 15 percent of the value of the mortgage loan for the first three years, contingent on loan performance, or a requirement to retain say 10 percent of the mortgage loan themselves for the life of the loan, subordinated to the buyers/owners of the rest of the mortgage loan, they would have been much more careful and discriminating in making the loans and the sub-prime mortgage loan crisis could have been largely avoided. Provisions such as these have been introduced in the recently proposed reform of financial regulation in the United States.

BIASED CREDIT RATING AGENCIES

Securitization without any residual liability encourages moral hazard on the part of the originating mortgage lenders. Ultimately the purchasers of these sub-prime mortgage loan-backed securities could only rely on the ratings given by the credit rating agencies on these securities. But the credit rating agencies also had no liabilities for mis-rating, but were compensated for providing ratings satisfactory to the issuers of these securities, creating yet another potential moral hazard. One of the problems is that a credit rating agency is nowadays paid by the firm it rates, but if the firm does not like the rating it receives from that particular credit rating agency, it does not have to pay but can go on to another credit agency until it finds one that will give it a satisfactory rating. But credit rating agencies want and need to be paid, and may therefore compromise their judgment (thus moral hazard once again). Hence, published credit ratings are likely to be biased upward. These credit ratings can therefore sometimes be worse than worthless. The information embodied in the credit rating is unreliable and misleading and give investors and potential investors a false sense of security.

EXCESSIVE LEVERAGE AND MORAL HAZARD

Excessive leverage also encourages moral hazard and high-risk-taking because it reduces the potential pain that may result from a loss. If a firm with net equity funds of $1 million operates with a debt-to-equity ratio of 50 to 1, a 10 percent return on assets (after interest payments) translates into a profit of $5 million and a 500 percent return on equity; but a -10 percent return on assets, which implies a loss of $5 million, will only result in an actual loss of $1 million to the shareholders of the firm (the firm will of course have negative net worth and be in bankruptcy). Thus, controlling excessive leverage also reduces risk-taking through reducing the incidence of moral hazard.

However, moral hazard, that is, "hidden action," and lack of full information disclosure, also help to enable excessive leverage. For example, by keeping potential liabilities off the balance sheet of a financial institution enables that financial institution to have a much higher actual leverage than otherwise allowed by the regulatory agencies. Similarly, "shadow banking" activities provide a camouflage to what are effectively "bank loans."

MORAL HAZARD OF INSURERS

It is well known that insurance is subject to moral hazard, that is, the insured may for other reasons undertake "hidden action" to trigger the insurance pay-off. For example, a person may be tempted to set fire to his or her own house, or to someone else's house on which he or she has taken out fire insurance, to collect the insurance proceeds. Excessive insurance or over-insurance, that is, insuring a property for more than its true market value, is an open invitation to the insured to trigger the insurance pay-off, as the insured can benefit more from the insurance pay-off than from maintaining the status quo. The insurance companies have learned from bitter past experience that this may happen, and generally will insure only those who have an insurable interest, for example, they will only sell insurance to the actual owner of a house, or to the bank with the mortgage loan, but not to others, and often to offer only less-than-full-market-value insurance (the insurance payoff is always with reference to the current market value). Less than full market-value insurance amounts to a form of co-payment and can discourage moral hazard. For example, if the insured of a house can only recover from insurance proceeds less than the full market value and hence will have not only no incentive to burn down his or her own house to collect the insurance, but in addition will also have the incentive to exercise due care for the house to prevent the occurrence of a fire.

TRANSACTION OF UNREGULATED CDSs

Credit default swaps (CDSs) are new financial instruments introduced in the late 1990s that are totally unregulated. In principle, they are insurance contracts on the bonds, the outstanding obligations, of a firm. The CDSs are sold by insurance companies and pay off in the event there is a default on the bonds by the bond-issuing firm. As indicated above, a fundamental principle of insurance is that the insured must have an insurable interest. Otherwise it would encourage moral hazard. (And moreover, to discourage moral hazard, insurance should be less than full.) Thus, for example, it is reasonable for someone who owns Lehman Brothers bonds, or who is a contractor or supplier owed money by Lehman Brothers, to purchase a CDS from American International Group, a US insurance company, up to the amount outstanding. But it is not reasonable for anyone else with no direct exposure to Lehman Brothers, especially if this person has the power to influence whether Lehman Brothers would go into bankruptcy, to purchase CDSs on Lehman Brothers, or to purchase an amount of CDS greater than the actual financial exposure.

Unfortunately, the insurance companies that sold CDSs lost sight of the fact that they were selling insurance. They thought they were just taking bets, like Ladbrokes, but even Ladbrokes does not itself take a position on a bet. Indiscriminate sale of credit default swaps (CDSs) is the principal cause of AIG's problems. It is like allowing many strangers to buy insurance on someone's house, creating an incentive for them to set fire to it and collect the insurance. Or a pirate buying insurance on someone else's ship from Lloyds and then sinking it to collect the insurance. This is the well known problem of moral hazard in insurance that every insurance company should know and avoid.

But AIG sold many times more CDSs on Lehman Brothers than Lehman Brothers had bonds outstanding (reportedly much more than ten times). Many purchasers of such CDSs were simply gambling on a Lehman Brothers failure. It would have been all right if these purchasers had no influence on whether Lehman Brothers would go under or not. Or if AIG does not take a position itself, merely squaring those who bet that Lehman Brothers would fail with those who bet Lehman Brothers would survive, letting the market determine the odds. Unfortunately, that is not the case. AIG took on the bets itself, and many of the purchasers of the CDSs had the power to help force Lehman Brothers under, for example, by massively shorting its stocks or bonds, so that Lehman Brothers would be effectively prevented from accessing the capital and credit markets.

A simple way to look at the problem of CDSs is to imagine everyone in the United Kingdom being allowed to buy fire insurance on Buckingham Palace, in addition to Her Majesty the Queen herself. There will be a strong incentive for those who have bought insurance and who do not have to live in Buckingham Palace to get together and try to burn it down, and collect the insurance. And the insurance company will then have to pay each insured individually the total value of Buckingham Palace, in addition to paying off Her Majesty, resulting in losses to the insurance company many times over the value of Buckingham Palace.

In retrospect, even considered as insurance, the CDSs on Lehman Brothers were not priced correctly. The price of the CDSs did not reflect adequately the probability of its failure, given its high degree of leverage and potential liabilities, and moreover did not take into account adverse selection—people buy insurance only because they have reason to expect that there is a high probability that they will be able to collect the insurance. Furthermore, the insurance industry is normally regulated by the government to ensure that the insurance companies have adequate reserves to pay the claims if and when they arise. However, CDSs were not regulated as insurance because the US Congress passed legislation in the late 1990s declaring that CDSs were neither insurance nor gaming, thus effectively enabling CDSs to escape possible government regulation and supervision altogether. Adequate insurance reserves were never properly established for CDSs. That is one reason why AIG was in so much trouble and required direct government assistance.

CDSs, if sold indiscriminately, can provide the instruments for a form of predatory speculation—hedge funds and other investors seek relatively weak firms, buy their CDSs and drive them into bankruptcy by selling short (often naked) their bonds and stocks. In retrospect, the availability of CDSs on Lehman Brothers actually increased the probability of failure of Lehman Brothers rather than decreased it, thus increasing rather than decreasing the overall riskiness of the financial sector and the economy.

One argument advanced by the supporters of unrestricted sales and trading of CDSs is that it may lower the cost of CDSs and therefore benefit the bond-holders who wish to hedge against a default of the bonds. But we must ask whether the owner of a house will allow others with no interest in his house to buy insurance on his house just because it may lower the cost of the insurance to the owner himself. The answer is obviously no, because it will create moral hazard for the other insured's, who will have a financial incentive for the house to be burned down. Another argument is that it will make the CDSs liquid—but why should the owner of a house need liquidity for his home insurance? His primary concerns should be to make sure that his insurance company is well capitalized and that no one else is allowed to buy insurance on his house.

MORAL HAZARD OF COMPENSATION SCHEMES

Another source of moral hazard is the asymmetric nature of the incentive compensation schemes at most US corporations and at many investment funds. These schemes typically provide for the executive/asset manager to reap huge rewards tied to the degree of successful performance over and above a certain benchmark (through stock options and "carry interest") but does not share in the losses (beyond possibly losing his or her job). These stock options and "carry interest", which allow an executive/asset manager to share the upside but not the downside, create moral hazard, appeal to their greed, and encourage him or her to take excessive risks and to focus only on the short term. Stock options, which provide only upside but no downside for the option grantees, are ideal for venture capital and for start-ups because these are inherently high-risk ventures but with really no down-side that is not already expected and will be shared by investors and executives alike. However, stock options may not be appropriate for mature firms because there may be a significant downside for the owners and shareholders of the firm which may not be shared by the executives granted the stock options. The high fees, including the cost of the so-called "carry interest," charged by the managers of investment funds, have the effect of motivating these asset managers to take excessive risk because they would share a significant proportion of the upside but not the downside.

Typically the fee structure of investment funds (including hedge funds and private equity funds) is 2 and 20—2 percent of the value of assets under management and 20 percent of the returns above a certain threshold, but the carry interest can go all the way up to as high as 44 percent. Such incentive schemes encourage risk-taking on the part of the asset manager because he or she stands to gain significantly if the fund makes it big but loses very little if the investment strategies fail. To be fair, there are asset managers who cap the upside of their fees, thus reducing their own incentive to take excessive risks. "Heads I win, tails you lose" is neither effective nor efficient as a method of incentive compensation for corporate executives and asset managers—it greatly encourages moral hazard and reckless and short-term oriented behavior.

Incentive compensation of senior executives should not be based on short-term results but instead should be based on long-term performance of the corporation, including the performance over a period after their retirement from the corporation. In this way they will have the incentive not to pursue quick short-term profits but to invest for long-term sustainable earnings as well as to help choose their successors carefully. An alternative is to require the executives/managers to own outright shares (through recourse loans from the corporation if necessary) in the corporation or the investment fund that constitute a high proportion of their personal net worth. That will help align their interests with those of the shareholders/investors and discourage moral hazard and excessive risk-taking.

"Too Big to Fail" Financial Institutions

Implicit guarantees of banks and financial institutions considered "too big to fail" by governments encourage moral hazard on the part of the large banks and financial institutions. Many of the largest financial institutions around the world took excessive risks with the belief that they would not fail and moreover would not be allowed to fail by their respective national governments. However, many of them did fail. The United States, the largest provider of international liquidity, is also itself in crisis, but it is really "too big to fail."

REINFORCING REGULATIONS AND OVERSIGHT

The global financial crisis was not inevitable. Unfortunately, the developed countries, or the regulators in the developed countries, failed to learn from their past mistakes. Markets do not and cannot function well automatically on their own. Regulation and supervision are essential for the well-functioning of the market—to maintain its competitive nature, to reduce information asymmetry, and to discourage moral hazard. The incentives are too strong for firms, if left alone, to try to monopolise markets or to otherwise benefit themselves at the expense of other market participants (e.g., front running, insider trading, market manipulation, spreading rumours, publishing false or misleading financial accounts, etc.). Excessive leverage also cannot be left to self-regulation. Information asymmetry can be reduced only through regulatory measures (there is no reason for an investor to disclose information voluntarily to one's potential competitors in the financial markets). Moral hazard must also be explicitly discouraged and controlled.

Strengthened financial regulation and supervision are therefore essential to avoid a recurrence of another financial crisis of similar magnitude to the current global financial crisis. What measures should be taken by financial regulatory and supervisory agencies to strengthen financial regulation and supervision? The following is a possible list:

(1) Restrain irrational exuberance
(2) Restrict excessive leverage
(3) Ensure competitiveness of markets
(4) Control moral hazard

The financial regulatory agencies should monitor asset (securities and property) markets and take appropriate measures to prevent asset price bubbles from becoming too big. In general, simply talking about "irrational exuberance" in the market is not enough to discourage speculators. Instruments that can be used by regulatory and supervisory agencies include controlling the loan to value ratios and loan ceilings in real estate markets and margin requirements in stock markets. Other instruments may include the pricing, quantity, and timing policies of public land sales and the pace of initial public offerings as well as more opportunistic additional public offerings through the use of "shelf registration," that is, pre-approved public offerings that can be activated at a time of the offering company's choice. The fundamental idea is to try to influence and modify long-term asset price expectations. If additional supplies are expected to be forthcoming in the future the asset price bubble cannot become too big.

Because of the negative externalities generated by excessive leverage, there is public interest in controlling the degree of leverage of firms, especially financial institutions. Excessive leverage should therefore be tightly controlled. Capital adequacy should be monitored. A firm is only "too big to fail" if it is heavily leveraged. If it is not heavily leveraged, it can be simply allowed to fail (the shareholders will lose but another firm or investor can take over its functions) but its failure will not have a devastating spillover effect on other firms and financial institutions. There should be restrictions on the degree of leverage in the economy, especially for the financial sector. Limits on leverage are easy to enforce and difficult to circumvent provided that off-balance-sheet activities are not allowed.

The regulatory and supervisory agencies should ensure competitiveness of the financial markets by reducing information asymmetry, increasing disclosure and transparency, and restricting dominant positions of market players. The public will be much better informed if off-balance-sheet activities are not allowed for publicly listed firms, including all financial institutions. This will also help to improve corporate governance, reduce actual leverage, and avoid negative surprises. The practice of "shadow banking," which leads to undisclosed "excessive leverage" and increases systemic uncertainty significantly should be prohibited—a bank should either make a direct loan to a corporation, or provide an explicit guarantee on the bonds and notes issued by the corporation, all of which will be explicitly on the balance sheet of the bank. At the current stage of financial development in many developing economies, allowing "shadow banking" will greatly increase systemic risk in these economies.

The introduction of the many new financial instruments has created additional problems for the regulators—instead of reducing and sharing risks, they concentrate and magnify risks and increase overall systemic risk. Many of these complex and non-standard financial instruments are priced and traded only privately (e.g., the "accumulator") and not on open public markets and exchanges. There is a crying need for simplification and standardization of financial derivatives and for them to be traded only on established and publicly regulated open exchanges. This assures some degree of transparency and fairer pricing, safeguards against market manipulation, and helps to reduce counter-party and systemic risks. Dominant positions (e.g., over 5 percent share of any specific traded financial instrument) in any financial market should be required to be disclosed, as well as any subsequent increases or decreases in such positions. In these instances, the final beneficial owners should also be disclosed to avoid the use of multiple names and accounts to circumvent the disclosure requirement. For certain instruments, there should be an upper limit to the market share that can be held by a single person or entity.

Moral hazard should be controlled and discouraged by the

regulators, so that any potential gain is accompanied by potential pain, reducing excessive risk-taking on the part of all market participants. This includes the regulation and supervision of the originating mortgage lenders, credit rating agencies, insurance companies and their products and business practices, as well as the degree of leverage of firms, including financial institutions and hedge funds. The goal is to reduce the incentive to take "hidden actions" and/or excessive risks.

LESSONS OF THE FINANCIAL CRISIS

If Credit Default Swaps (CDSs) were to be introduced in the developing economies such as China at all, they should be sold to only bona fide owners of the underlying bonds. And once the original owners sell the bonds, they should not be allowed to keep the CDSs—they will either have to be sold, with the bonds, to the new buyer, or they should be returned to the insurance company for a refund, if any.

If any bank or financial institution cuts corners, its costs will be lower and its profits will be higher. If the regulator allows a bank or financial institution to cut corners, other banks will be forced to follow in order to compete. Thus, in order to reduce systemic risk, financial regulation and supervision must be uniformly enforced. It is most important for the regulator not to allow bad practices gradually become industry-wide standard practices. Regulations must be clear and enforcement must be strict. Otherwise all the grey areas will appear white in no time. The regulatory agencies should always remember that their primary responsibility is the protection of consumers (depositors and borrowers), creditors and investors, ensuring the fairness and efficiency of the markets, and the security and stability of the financial system as a whole. It is not their responsibility to assure the profitability of the firms they are charged to regulate.

As the Chinese and other developing economies continue their rapid growth and "financial deepening," they must continue to strengthen their regulatory and supervisory capacities to deal with new situations and new financial instruments. They must learn from the lessons of the past mistakes made by regulatory agencies both domestically and abroad. The competitive market system has many advantages but it must meet certain conditions in order for it to produce economically efficient outcomes. The market left to its own cannot ensure that these conditions are met. Thus, regulatory and supervisory oversight continues to be important for China and other developing economies. The "visible hand" and the "invisible hand" must work together, hand in hand.

HUMAN PROPENSITY FOR GREED

Economics as a social science can play a useful role in providing analyses of the causes of the financial crisis, the lessons that can be drawn, possible remedial actions, and measures to prevent a recurrence of the financial crisis in the future.

In addition, there is, in some countries, an over-emphasis on monetary compensation as motivation and incentive, appealing only to the human nature of greed. I believe that at the most senior levels of management, it is not enough to use monetary incentives or short-term monetary performance indicators alone, nor is it desirable for a firm or organization to employ someone who is solely motivated by personal financial gain. Greed is often the underlying motivation for "hidden actions," for taking advantage of openings for moral hazard.

One good yardstick of the degree of "greed" is to look at the ratio of the highest-paid individual to the lowest-paid individual in a firm. In Japan, it is on average no more than ten to one, perhaps even less. In the United States, it is often one hundred to one, or more, and frequently based on the short-term performance of the price of the common stock. A compensation system which basically provides for "heads I win, tails you lose," and almost instantaneous gain encourages moral hazard, recklessness, and short-term opportunistic behavior, to the detriment of the other shareholders and stakeholders. However, "greed" is a social and cultural phenomenon. How much wealth should be considered enough? That depends fundamentally on the value system of a society, which in turn depends on its culture and traditions. One cannot change the prevailing compensation system of a country or region overnight—it is a function of its culture, traditions, and values and evolves very gradually.

The responsibility for the occurrence of the global financial crisis probably lies mostly with the regulatory and supervisory agencies in the developed countries, which failed to do their job. I have already provided some suggestions for strengthening regulation and supervision previously, for example, reducing excessive leverage, controlling moral hazard, and reducing information asymmetry. For the society as a whole, a longer-term perspective should be encouraged and greed should be suitably restrained. And people should be educated to realize that what is too good to be true is too good to be true.

Selected Works
Daisaku Ikeda

Choose Life with Arnold Toynbee. London: I.B. Tauris & Co. Ltd, 2007.

A Forum for Peace: Daisaku Ikeda's Proposals to the UN. London: I.B. Tauris & Co. Ltd, 2014.

Into Full Flower: Making Peace Cultures Happen with Elise Boulding. Cambridge, Mass.: Dialogue Path Press, 2010.

Knowing Our Worth: Conversations on Energy and Sustainability with Ernst Ulrich von Weizsacker. Cambridge, Mass.: Dialogue Path Press, 2016.

A Lifelong Quest for Peace with Linus Pauling. London: I.B. Tauris & Co. Ltd, 2009.

A New Humanism: The University Addresses of Daisaku Ikeda. London: I.B. Tauris & Co. Ltd, 2010.

Our World To Make: Hinduism, Buddhism, and the Rise of Global Civil Society with Ved Nanda. Cambridge, Mass.: Dialogue Path Press, 2015.

Planetary Citizenship with Hazel Henderson. Santa Monica, Calif.: Middleway Press, 2004.

A Quest for Global Peace with Joseph Rotblat. London: I.B. Tauris & Co. Ltd, 2007.

APPENDIX 7

Selected Works
Lawrence Lau

The Chinese Economy in the Twenty-First Century: An Econometric Approach. Singapore: World Scientific Publishing Company, 2006.

Econometrics and the Cost of Capital: Essays in Honor of Dale W. Jorgenson. Editor and contributor. Cambridge, Mass.: The M.I.T. Press, 2000.

Farmer Education and Farm Efficiency with Dean T. Jamison. Baltimore, Maryland: Johns Hopkins University Press, 1982.

Models of Development: A Comparative Study of Economic Growth in South Korea and Taiwan, revised and expanded edition. Editor and contributor. San Francisco, Calif.: ICS Press, 1990.

North Korea in Transition: Prospects for Economic and Social Reform with Chang-Ho Yoon. Northampton, Mass.: American Enterprise Institute, 2001.

U.S. Direct Investment in China with K. C. Fung and Joseph S. Lee. Washington, D.C.: American Enterprise Institute, 2004

Notes

CONVERSATION ONE
ECONOMICS FOR THE PEOPLE

1. In 2000, the university conferred an honorary doctorate of social science upon Mr. Ikeda.
2. The Institute of Oriental Studies of the Russian Academy of Sciences is a research institution founded in 1818 that covers the countries and cultures of Asia and North Africa. In 2007, after this exhibition, the St. Petersburg branch moved to Moscow and was reorganized into a separate Institute of Oriental Manuscripts.
3. This earthquake, often referred to in Japan as the Great East Japan Earthquake, struck about 43 miles off Japan's eastern coast on Friday, March 11, 2011. It triggered tsunamis as high as 130 feet, which travelled inland up to six miles in Japan's Tohoku and Sendai areas. There were reported to be 15,883 deaths and 2,667 missing throughout twenty-two prefectures.
4. East Asian currency crisis: In 1997, the government of Thailand, because it lacked sufficient foreign currency, was forced to float the value of the *baht*, previously tied to the value of the US dollar. This caused a cascading pattern of currency devaluation across Southeast Asia, especially in Indonesia and South Korea, causing steep market declines, reduced import revenue, and government turmoil. The World Bank and International Monetary Fund stepped in to limit the damage and keep it from spreading globally.
5. A subprime loan is a housing loan offered at a rate above prime

when borrowers do not qualify for prime rate loans. Consequently, subprime borrowers are often turned away from traditional lenders because of their low credit rating or other factors that suggest they are likely to default on the loan.

6. Greece's government debt crisis catapulted to global awareness in 2010. Billions of dollars in bailouts were provided, but went primarily to paying Greece's international loans. As part of this bailout, Greece was required to initiate extreme changes, including raising taxes and cutting pensions, which significantly affected Greece's middle class. See "Explaining Greece's Debt Crisis," June 17, 2016, *New York Times*, http://www.nytimes.com/interactive/2016/business/international/greece-debt-crisis-euro.html.

7. "Real economy" is the part of the economy concerned with actually producing goods and services, in contrast to those parts of the economy concerned with buying and selling on the financial markets.

CONVERSATION TWO
HONG KONG'S POTENTIAL

1. The authors conducted their dialogue during 2014.
2. HKSGI refers to the Soka Gakkai International of Hong Kong, http://www.hksgi.org/eng/.
3. China currently has two Special Administrative Regions, as legislated by Article 31 of the Constitution of the People's Republic of China in 1982. They are Hong Kong and Macau. Each has its own political system separate from the PRC, its own chief executive, and operates under a capitalist economy.
4. For 2012 results of the Programme for International Student Assessment, see http://www.oecd.org/pisa/keyfindings/pisa-2012-results.htm.
5. Also published in Japan, the work garnered considerable attention and controversy as it shed light on both the positive and negative aspects of the strict, intense approach of Chinese parents when educating their children.
6. Larry Hickman, Jim Garrison, and Daisaku Ikeda, *Living As Learning: John Dewey in the 21st Century* (Cambridge, Mass.: Dialogue Path Press, 2014), p. 117.
7. Ibid., p. 116.

8. Translated from Japanese. See Mika Yamada, *Kokyoiku to kodomo no seikatsu o tsunagu honkon taiwan no kyoiku kaikaku* (Educational Reform in Hong Kong and Taiwan Linking Public Education to Children's Lives) (Nagoya: Fubaisha, 2011), p. 189.

9. See "World University Rankings 2008" in *Times Higher Education* and QS Quacquarelli Symonds, https://www.timeshighereducation.com/sites/default/files/Attachments/THE/THE/17_August_2007/attachments/WORLDRANKINGS2008.pdf.

10. Putonghua: Also known as Modern Standard Mandarin, Standard Mandarin, or simply Mandarin, it is the sole official language of both China and Taiwan, and also one of the four official languages of Singapore.

11. Sponsored by the Hong Kong Schools Music and Speech Association.

12. The Project for Promotion of Global Human Resource Development, http://www.jsps.go.jp/j-gjinzai/data/shinsa/h24/H24_gjinzai_kekka_e.pdf.

13. The American Association for the Advancement of Science, "Internationalization of University Education in Japan" (Washington, D.C.: Science/AAAS Custom Publishing Office, 2015), p. 1493.

14. Translated from Japanese. Daisaku Ikeda, *Ikeda Daisaku zenshu* (The Complete Works of Daisaku Ikeda), vol. 2 (Tokyo: Seikyo Shimbunsha, 1999), pp. 342–43.

CONVERSATION THREE
SUCCESSFUL HIGHER EDUCATION

1. This statement appears in the *Seikyo Shimbun*, the Soka Gakkai daily newspaper, on September 28, 1991.

2. Karl Jaspers, *The Idea of the University*, ed. K. W. Deutsch and trans. H. A. T. Reiche and H. F. Vanderschmidt (Boston: Beacon Press, 1959), p. 45.

3. Jean-Jacques Rousseau, *Emile; or On Education*, trans. Allan Bloom (London: Penguin Books, 1991), p. 49.

4. Also known as the Mukden Incident. On September 18, 1931, a Japanese officer caused a small explosion close to a railway line owned by Japan's South Manchuria Railway near the town of Mukden (now Shenyang). The Imperial Japanese Army blamed Chinese dissidents for the explosion and proceeded to occupy Manchuria, establishing

the puppet state of Manchukuo six months later. Japan's ruse was soon exposed to the international community, leading to Japan's diplomatic isolation and its March 1933 withdrawal from the League of Nations.

5. Control Yuan is one of five branches of the government of the Republic of China and monitors the other four branches, similar to the Government Accountability Office of the United States.

6. Nichiren (1222–1282) is the Buddhist priest and reformer whose teachings form the basis of Nichiren Buddhism. He often wrote in a dialogic format and submitted this treatise to Hojo Tokiyori, a retired regent but still the most powerful figure in Japan's ruling clan, on July 16, 1260, to remonstrate with the regime's misguided beliefs. Nichiren called for the betterment of society through Buddhist teachings that he believed were most appropriate for the times. See Nichiren, *The Writings of Nichiren Daishonin*, vol. 1 (Tokyo: Soka Gakkai, 1999), pp. 6–30.

7. The Hong Kong riots of 1966 were triggered by the British colonial government's decision to increase the fare of the Star Ferry, an important means to carry people back and forth from the island of Hong Kong to Kowloon Peninsula. One person died in three days of rioting, and more than 1,800 were arrested. In 1967, the Hong Kong Leftist riots originated as a minor labor dispute that grew into large-scale demonstrations against British colonial rule.

8. *Gaigé kaifang*: Literally, "reform and opening," also referred to as the Chinese economic reform. It is the program of economic reforms in the People's Republic of China that started in December 1978, led by reformists in the Communist Party of China, which was headed by Deng Xiaoping.

9. Translated from Japanese. "*Keiai suru honkon no tomo ni okuru: eiko no toshi honkon no kyokujitsu*" (At the Dawn of Hong Kong, the City of Enduring Glory—to My Beloved Friends in Hong Kong), which appears in the *Seikyo Shimbun* on February 24, 1997.

Conversation Four
The Joy of Learning

1. See https://www.whitehouse.gov/1600/presidents/johnfkennedy.

2. The Soka school system, founded by Daisaku Ikeda in 1968, is based on Soka education. The Soka Junior and Senior High Schools—

established by President Ikeda in Kodaira, Tokyo—were the first institutions to be established. The system now includes kindergartens, elementary, junior and senior high schools, a university in Hachioji, Tokyo, and a university in Aliso Viejo, Calif. Kindergartens have been established in Hong Kong, Singapore, Malaysia, South Korea, and Brazil.

3. Daisaku Ikeda, *The Human Revolution* (Santa Monica, Calif.: World Tribune Press, 2004), Book 2, pp. 820–23.

4. Ibid., pp. 823–25.

5. Liu Bei, better known as Xuande, founded the Kingdom of Shu and was regarded as a great statesman and strategist in the Three Kingdoms Period (220–80).

6. Cao Cao, better known as Mengde, laid the foundations of the Kingdom of Wei and was regarded as one of the greatest warlords at the end of the Han dynasty of China.

7. Arnold J. Toynbee, *A Study of History*, vol. 10 (London: Oxford University Press, 1954), p. 213.

8. Translated from Japanese. Goro Yoshizawa, *Toinbi: hito to shiso*, vol. 69 (Toynbee: The Man and His Vision) (Tokyo: Shimizu Shoin, 1982), p. 29.

CONVERSATION FIVE
THE PATH OF FRIENDSHIP

1. Mr. Ikeda visited Fudan University in 1975, 1978, and 1984. In 1984, he was awarded an honorary professorship by the university. On that occasion, he delivered an address, "The Making of History," on traditional Chinese views of history. See *A New Humanism: The University Addresses of Daisaku Ikeda* (London and New York: I.B. Tauris, 2010) pp. 97–100.

2. Fudan Public School: The Chinese character for *fu* connotes "revival," expressing Yu Youren's hope to revive China, and the Chinese character for *dan* is a direct reference to the name of Ma Xiangbo's previous school, Zhendan Xueyuan.

3. Translated from Japanese. Gishin Nishide, *Kinsen fundo no gotoshi* (Money Is Like Dung) (Tokyo: Shodo Geijutsu-sha, 2012), pp. 249–320.

4. Mozi, *The Ethical and Political Works of Mozi*, trans. Mei Yi-pao (London: Arthur Probsthain, 1929), p. 195.

5. *The Lotus Sutra and Its Opening and Closing Sutras,* trans. Burton Watson (Tokyo: Soka Gakkai, 2009), p. 70.

6. Nam-myoho-renge-kyo: Literally, "Devotion to the Lotus Sutra of the Wonderful Law." The ultimate law or truth of the universe, according to Nichiren's teachings. Nichiren identifies it with the universal law or principle implicit in the meaning of the Lotus Sutra. (*The Soka Gakkai Dictionary of Buddhism* [Tokyo: Soka Gakkai, 2002], p. 424)

7. The Gohonzon, a scroll inscribed with Chinese characters and sometimes compared to a spiritual mirror, is the object of fundamental respect in Nichiren Buddhism. SGI members enshrine the Gohonzon in Buddhist altars in their homes as a focal point for the daily practice of chanting Nam-myoho-renge-kyo and reciting portions of the Lotus Sutra.

8. Nichiren, *The Writings of Nichiren Daishonin,* vol. I (Tokyo: Soka Gakkai, 1999), p. 412.

9. One of the three assemblies described in the Lotus Sutra, in which the entire gathering of listeners is suspended in space above this world. The account of the ceremony extends from the "Treasure Tower" to the "Entrustment" chapters of the sutra. At its heart is the revelation of the Buddha's original enlightenment in the remote past and the transfer of the essence of the sutra to the Bodhisattvas of the Earth. (See *The Lotus Sutra and Its Opening and Closing Sutras* [Tokyo: Soka Gakkai, 2009].)

10. Bodhisattvas: Those who aspire to enlightenment. *Bodhi* means enlightenment, and *sattva,* a living being. In Nichiren Buddhism, this is a state characterized by compassion in which one seeks enlightenment both for oneself and others. In this state, one finds satisfaction in devoting oneself to relieving the suffering of others and leading them to happiness. (*The Soka Gakkai Dictionary of Buddhism* [Tokyo: Soka Gakkai, 2002], pp. 48–49)

11. The Latter Day of the Law —the last of the three periods following a Buddha's death, when Buddhism falls into confusion and its teachings lose the power to lead people to enlightenment. The Latter Day of the Law of Shakyamuni Buddha is said to last for ten thousand years and more. In Japan it was believed that the Latter Day had begun in 1052. Many Treasures is a Buddha who, in the Lotus Sutra, appears seated within the treasure tower at the Ceremony in the Air

to bear witness to the veracity of Shakyamuni Buddha's teachings. (*The Writings of Nichiren Daishonin*, vol. I, p. 299)

12. Ibid., p. 386.

13. Translated from Japanese. Interview with Dr. Marinoff, *Seikyo Shimbun*, September 26, 2002.

14. In *The Book of Kindred Sayings*, the disciple Ananda asks Shakyamuni, "Having good friends and practicing among them would be halfway to the mastery of the Buddha Way, would it not?" Shakyamuni replies: "Having good friends does not constitute the midpoint to the Buddha Way. It constitutes all of the Buddha Way" (trans. F. L. Woodward, p. 2).

15. *The Writings of Nichiren Daishonin*, vol. 1, p. 463.

16. Ibid., p. 385.

17. Arnold Toynbee, *A Historian's Approach to Religion* (Oxford: Oxford University Press, 1979), p. 262.

18. In 1983, Daisaku Ikeda began submitting peace proposals annually to the United Nations on January 26, the anniversary of the founding of the Soka Gakkai International in 1975. These proposals offer perspectives on critical issues facing humanity, suggesting solutions and responses grounded in Buddhist humanism. They also put forth specific agendas for strengthening the United Nations, including avenues for the involvement of civil society. (See ed. Olivier Urbain, *A Forum for Peace: Daisaku Ikeda's Proposals to the UN* [London: I.B. Tauris, 2014].)

19. See December 1968 *Gekkan Ajia* (Asia Monthly).

20. Translated from Japanese. Daisaku Ikeda, *Ikeda Daisaku zenshu* (The Complete Works of Daisaku Ikeda), vol. 118 (Tokyo: Seikyo Shimbun-sha, 2000), p. 208.

21. Arnold Toynbee and Daisaku Ikeda, *Choose Life* (London: I.B. Tauris, 2007), p. 221.

CONVERSATION SIX
PROSPECTS FOR EAST ASIA

1. Translated from Japanese. Richard Coudenhove-Kalergi and Daisaku Ikeda, *Bunmei nishi to higashi* (Civilization, East and West) (Tokyo: Seikyo Shimbun-sha, 1975), p. 39.

2. Eurozone crisis: Also referred to as the European debt crisis. A debt

crisis that has been unfolding in the European Union since the end of 2009. Some member states (including Ireland, Cyprus, Greece, Portugal, and Spain) have been unable to repay or refinance their government debt or to bail out banks without the assistance of a third party.

3. The March 11, 2011, earthquake and tsunami in Tohoku, Japan, caused equipment failures leading to the Fukushima Daiichi nuclear disaster (specifically, three nuclear meltdowns and the release of radioactive materials) beginning on March 12. It is considered the largest nuclear disaster since the 1986 Chernobyl disaster, and the second disaster (after Chernobyl) to be given the Level 7 event classification of the International Nuclear Event Scale, releasing an estimated 10 to 30 percent of the radiation of the Chernobyl accident.

4. Daisaku Ikeda, "Building Global Solidarity Toward Nuclear Abolition," in *A Forum for Peace*, pp. 311–42.

5. The disputed islands are the Senkaku Islands in Japan and the Diaoyo Islands in China. Even though the islands are uninhabited, they are close to important shipping lanes, potential oil and gas reserves, and rich fishing areas. They also are considered strategically located for military reasons.

6. The ASEAN Regional Forum was established as a result of agreements reached at the Twenty-sixth ASEAN Ministerial Meeting and Post Ministerial Conference, held in Singapore July 23–25, 1993. The inaugural meeting of the ARF was held in Bangkok on July 25, 1994. The objectives of the forum are to foster constructive dialogue and consultation on political and security issues of common interest and concern, and to make significant contributions to efforts toward confidence-building and preventive diplomacy in the Asia-Pacific region. The current participants in the ARF are: Australia, Bangladesh, Brunei Darussalam, Cambodia, Canada, China, the European Union, India, Indonesia, Japan, Laos, Malaysia, Mongolia, Myanmar, New Zealand, North Korea, Pakistan, Papua New Guinea, the Philippines, Russia, Singapore, South Korea, Sri Lanka, Thailand, Timor-Leste, the United States, and Vietnam.

7. See Matthias Vanhullebusch, "Finance, Rule of Law and Human Rights in China" in *Finance, Rule of Law and Development in Asia*, eds. Jiaxing Hu, Matthias Vanhullebusch, and Andrew Harding (Leiden, the Netherlands: Brill/Nijhoff, 2016), p. 169.

CONVERSATION SEVEN
LEARNING AS GROWTH

1. Tsunesaburo Makiguchi, *Education for Creative Living: Ideas and Proposals of Tsunesaburo Makiguchi*, trans. Alfred Birnbaum and ed. Dayle M. Bethel (Ames, Iowa: Iowa State University Press, 1989), p. 168.
2. Lu Xun, *Selected Works*, vol. 4, trans. Yang Xianyi and Gladys Yang (Beijing: Foreign Language Press, 1985), pp. 299–300.
3. See "Most International Students," accessed July 29, 2014, http://colleges.usnews.rankingsandreviews.com/best-colleges/rankings/national-liberal-arts-colleges/most-international.
4. See "Most Students Studying Abroad," accessed November 19, 2015, http://colleges.usnews.rankingsandreviews.com/best-colleges/rankings/most-study-abroad.
5. Chinese University of Hong Kong. Communications and Public Relations Office, "Installation of the New Vice-Chancellor: Address by Professor Lawrence J. Lau, BS, MA, PhD, DSSc (Hon)." Press release on December 9, 2004, http://www.cuhk.edu.hk/cpr/pressrelease/041209VCspeech_e.htm.
6. Vincent Harding and Daisaku Ikeda, *America Will Be! Conversations on Hope, Freedom, and Democracy* (Cambridge, Mass: Dialogue Path Press, 2013), p. 12.
7. Ibid., p. 14.
8. Ibid., pp. 4–5.
9. Translated from Japanese. Report of personal meeting between President Ikeda and Mr. Lau on January 16, 2007, published in the *Seikyo Shimbun* on February 8, 2007.
10. Ibid.
11. Johann Wolfgang von Goethe, *From My Life: Poetry and Truth—Parts One to Three* in *Goethe's Collected Works*, vol. 4, trans. Robert R. Heitner and eds. Thomas P. Saine and Jeffrey L. Sammons (Princeton, NJ: Princeton University Press, 1987), p. 246.

CONVERSATION EIGHT
ECONOMICS FOR HAPPINESS

1. Deng Xiaoping traveled to Wuhan, Shenzhen, Zhuhai, Shanghai, and other cities in south China, declaring his commitment to reforms and liberalization, and to accelerating economic development.
2. Throughout 1989, students in Beijing led demonstrations in support of greater democracy in China, sometimes called the '89 Democracy Movement. On June 4, government troops killed several protesters who sought to block the military's advance to Tiananmen Square. The number of civilian deaths is estimated between several hundred to thousands. The event drew international condemnation. Investors withdrew money from China, and several Western countries enforced economic sanctions and embargoes, forcing China to begin a long process of attempting to move beyond its reputation as a repressive regime. In China the tragedy is known by its date as the June Fourth Incident, and in the West it is known by its location as the Tiananmen Square Massacre.
3. Translated from Japanese. John Kenneth Galbraith, *Nihon keizai e no saigo no keikoku* (The Last Warning to the Japanese Economy), trans. Takashi Kakuma (Tokyo: Tokuma Shoten, 2002), p. 16.
4. *Inaugural Addresses of the Presidents of the United States: Grover Cleveland (1885) to Barack H. Obama (2009)* (Bedford, Mass.: Applewood Books, 2009), p. 93.
5. International Labor Organization report, "Global Employment Trends 2014: The Risk of a Jobless Recovery," http://www.ilo.org/global/research/global-reports/global-employment-trends/2014/WCMS_233953/lang--en/index.htm.
6. Daisaku Ikeda, "Compassion, Wisdom and Courage: Building a Global Society of Peace and Creative Coexistence," 2013 peace proposal, http://www.sgi.org/content/files/about-us/president-ikedas-proposals/peaceproposal2013.pdf.
7. Translated from Japanese. Tsunesaburo Makiguchi, *Jinsei chirigaku* (A Geography of Human Life) in *Makiguchi Tsunesaburo zenshu* (The Complete Works of Tsunesaburo Makiguchi), vol. 1 (Tokyo: Daisanbunmei-sha, 1983), p. 218.
8. See http://www.reinisfischer.com/gdp-brics-countries-2013.
9. Translated from Japanese. Victor A. Sadovnichy and Daisaku Ikeda,

Asu no sekai kyoiku no shimei—nijuisseiki no ningen o kosatsu suru (The Mission of Education in Tomorrow's World—Thoughts on Humanity in the 21st Century) (Tokyo: Ushio Publishing Co., Ltd., 2013), p. 130.

10. Ibid., p. 126.
11. Translated from Japanese. Victor A. Sadovnichy and Daisaku Ikeda, *Gaku wa hikari—bunmei to kyoiku no mirai o kataru* (The Illuminating Power of Learning—Dialogue on the Future of Culture and Education) (Tokyo: Ushio Publishing Co., Ltd., 2004), pp. 220–21.
12. Ibid., pp. 224–25.
13. Sadovnichy and Ikeda, *Asu no sekai*, p. 120.

APPENDIX 1: PROPOSAL FOR THE NORMALIZATION OF JAPAN-CHINA RELATIONS

1. Republic of China is commonly known as "Taiwan." Even official government references use variously "Republic of China (Taiwan)" or "Republic of China/Taiwan" or "Taiwan (ROC)." It was a member of the United Nations from its inception (1945) until 1971, when China (PRC) took over the seat.

APPENDIX 2: BONDS OF BILATERAL FRIENDSHIP MUST NEVER BE BROKEN

1. Daisaku Ikeda, *A New Humanism*, p. 17.

APPENDIX 3: REGIONAL COOPERATION FOR RESILIENCE

1. World Meteorlogical Organization, "2001–2010, A Decade of Climate Extremes." Press release, July 3, 2013. See https://www.wmo.int/pages/mediacentre/press_releases/pr_976_en.html.
2. Intergovernmental Panel on Climate Change, *Managing the Risks of Extreme Events and Disasters to Advance Climate Change Adaptation* (New York: Cambridge University Press, 2012), p. 269.
3. United Nations University, "Loss and Damage from Climate Change Already Happening: UNU Report." News on November 13, 2013. See http://unu.edu/media-relations/releases/loss-and-damage-from-

climate-change-is-already-happening-says-unu-report.html#info.

4. Andrew Holland and Xander Vagg, "The Global Security Defense Index on Climate Change: National Security Perspectives on Climate Change from Around the World." Preliminary Results on March 21, 2013, https://americansecurityproject.org/ASP%20Reports/Ref%20 0121%20-%20Global%20Security%20Defense%20Index%20 P-Results.pdf.

5. Translated from Japanese. Kevin P. Clements and Daisaku Ikeda, "*Heiwa no seiki e—minshu no chosen*" (Towards Creating a Century of Peace: Challenges of the People) in the March 2014 issue of *The Ushio* (Tokyo: Ushio Publishing Co., Ltd., 2014), p. 197.

6. Joseph E. Stiglitz, *Global Public Goods: International Cooperation in the 21st Century*, eds. Inge Kaul, Isabelle Grunberg, and Marc A. Stern (New York: Oxford University Press, 1999), p. 308.

7. Thomas Jefferson, *The Writings of Thomas Jefferson*, vol. 6, ed. Henry Augustine Washington (New York: H.W. Derby, 1861), p. 180.

8. Translated from Japanese. Tsunesaburo Makiguchi, *Jinsei chirigaku* (A Geography of Human Life) in *Makiguchi Tsunesaburo zenshu* (The Complete Works of Makiguchi Tsunesaburo), vol. 2 (Tokyo: Daisanbunmei-sha, 1996), p. 399.

APPENDIX 4: SHARING IN BEST PRACTICES FOR HUMAN TALENT DEVELOPMENT

1. Jean Monnet, *Memoirs*, trans. Richard Mayne (London: Collins, 1976), p. 323.

2. Guido Westerwelle and Laurent Fabius, "Germany and France at the Service of Europe," report from Le Monde et al., January 22, 2013, http://www.franceintheus.org/spip.php?article4242.

3. Translated from Japanese. Sakuzo Yoshino, *Yoshino Sakuzo senshu* (Selected Works of Sakuzo Yoshino), vol. 8 (Tokyo: Iwanami Shoten, 1996), pp. 218–19.

Index

About the Authors

LAWRENCE J. LAU was Professor of Economics at Stanford University from 1976 until 2004, when he became sixth Vice Chancellor of the Chinese University of Hong Kong, serving in that position for seven years. Dr. Lau was born in Zunyi in Guizhou Province, China, in 1944. He received his primary and secondary education in Hong Kong. He gained his bachelor's of science degree from Stanford University and his master's and doctorate degrees in economics from the University of California, Berkeley, specializing in economic development and the economies of East Asia, including that of China. In 1966, he developed the first econometric model of China and continued improving the model. During his time at Stanford, he served as a co-director of the Asia-Pacific Research Center at Stanford University and director of the Stanford Institute for Economic Policy Research. Currently, he is a member of the twelfth National Committee of the Chinese People's Political Consultative Conference and Vice Chairman of its Subcommittee of Economics, and is a fellow and member of several other international economics associations. He has authored such works as *The Chinese Economy in the Twenty-first Century: An Econometric Approach*, and published more than 170 articles and notes in international professional journals.

DAISAKU IKEDA is president of the Soka Gakkai International, a lay Buddhist organization with more than twelve million members worldwide. He has written and lectured widely on Buddhism, humanism, and global ethics. More than fifty of his dialogues have been published, including *Choose Life* with Arnold J. Toynbee, *Moral Lessons of the Twentieth Century* with Mikhail Gorbachev, *A*

Quest for Global Peace with Joseph Rotblat, *New Horizons in Eastern Humanism* with Tu Weiming, and *America Will Be!: Conversations on Hope, Freedom, and Democracy* with Vincent Harding. Dedicated to education that promotes humanistic ideals, Mr. Ikeda founded Soka University in Tokyo in 1971 and, in 2001, Soka University of America in Aliso Viejo, California. In furtherance of his vision of fostering dialogue and solidarity for peace, Mr. Ikeda has founded three independent, nonprofit research institutes: the Ikeda Center for Peace, Learning, and Dialogue, the Toda Institute for Global Peace and Policy Research, and the Institute of Oriental Philosophy. He has received many academic honors, including the United Nations Peace Award in 1983.

Titles from Dialogue Path Press
All titles co-authored by Daisaku Ikeda

KNOWING OUR WORTH: CONVERSATIONS ON ENERGY AND SUS-
TAINABILITY (2016) *On healing the planet and moving toward
an environmentally sustainable future.* With Ernst Ulrich von
Weizsäcker, former Dean, Donald Bren School of Environmen-
tal Science and Management, University of California, Santa
Barbara, and co-president of the Club of Rome

OUR WORLD TO MAKE: HINDUISM, BUDDHISM, AND THE RISE
OF GLOBAL CIVIL SOCIETY (2015) *Presenting a vision for the
future of a global civil society based on our shared humanity.* With
Ved Nanda, Evans University Professor and Thompson G.
Marsh Professor of Law, University of Denver

LIVING AS LEARNING: JOHN DEWEY IN THE 21ST CENTURY
(2014) *Exploring the contemporary, cross-cultural relevance of
John Dewey's philosophy of education.* With Jim Garrison, Professor of Philosophy of Education, Virginia Tech University
And Larry A. Hickman, Director, Center for Dewey Studies, and Professor of Philosophy, Southern Illinois University
Carbondale

THE ART OF TRUE RELATIONS: CONVERSATIONS ON THE PO-
ETIC HEART OF HUMAN POSSIBILITY (2014) *Illuminating the
bonds that form the foundation of the human experience.* With
Sarah Wider, Professor of English and Women's Studies, Col-
gate University

AMERICA WILL BE!: CONVERSATIONS ON HOPE, FREEDOM, AND
DEMOCRACY (2013) *Insightful perspectives on the unfolding of the*

American civil rights movement. With Vincent Harding, author and confidant of Martin Luther King Jr., and chairperson of the Veterans of Hope Project, Iliff School of Theology

THE INNER PHILOSOPHER: CONVERSATIONS ON PHILOSOPHY'S TRANSFORMATIVE POWER (2012) *An empowering look at the wisdom and practical application of philosophy.* With Lou Marinoff, Professor and Chair of Philosophy, The City College of New York

INTO FULL FLOWER: MAKING PEACE CULTURES HAPPEN (2010) *Two peace activists shed light on the process of peace building.* With Elise M. Boulding, Professor of Sociology Emerita, Dartmouth College

CREATING WALDENS: AN EAST-WEST CONVERSATION ON THE AMERICAN RENAISSANCE (2009) *An exploration of the spiritual and ethical insights of Emerson, Thoreau, and Whitman.* With Ronald A. Bosco, Distinguished Professor of English and American Literature, University at Albany, State University of New York And Joel Myerson, Carolina Distinguished Professor of American Literature, Emeritus, University of South Carolina